透视
Perception

简悦 刘洁莹 编译

文化 是一种选择
既可做高远的 透视
亦可做深刻的反省
每一条不同的去向与路径
有不同的风景可堪回味

高端导读版
［文化卷］

天津教育出版社

图书在版编目(CIP)数据

透视／简悦,刘洁莹编译.—天津：天津教育出版社,2012.1
（美丽英文：高端导读版）
ISBN 978-7-5309-6639-6

Ⅰ.①透… Ⅱ.①简… ②刘… Ⅲ.①英语—汉语—对照读物 ②随笔—作品集—世界 Ⅳ.①H319.4：I

中国版本图书馆 CIP 数据核字（2011）第 268268 号

美丽英文·高端导读版　透视

出 版 人	胡振泰
编　　译	简　悦　刘洁莹
选题策划	袁　颖　王艳超
责任编辑	王艳超
装帧设计	郭亚非
出版发行	天津教育出版社 天津市和平区西康路 35 号　邮政编码 300051 http://www.tjeph.com.cn
经　　销	新华书店
印　　刷	天津新华二印刷有限公司
版　　次	2012 年 1 月第 1 版
印　　次	2012 年 1 月第 1 次印刷
规　　格	16 开（787mm×1092mm）
字　　数	120 千字
印　　张	12.5
定　　价	24.00 元

Content

Shakespeare Had No BlackBerry and Aristotle Managed Without an iPhone / 001
莎翁没有"黑莓",亚里士多德也没有"苹果"

Walking on the Moon—Michael Jackson in Motion / 007
月球漫步——舞动的迈克尔·杰克逊

South Park Has a Silent Partner / 013
《南方公园》那位沉默的合伙人

Brand Loyalty / 019
品牌忠诚

Angry Birds, Flocking to Cellphones Everywhere / 025
愤怒的小鸟,蜂拥飞至各地手机

London Designers Hail "Elegant" Kate Middleton / 031
英伦设计师盛赞优雅凯特

A Classroom Tool for Opening up Shakespeare: The Sitcom / 037
了解莎翁的新方式——情景喜剧

Lo' and Behold / 044
看那些名牌!

Man United! / 050
男人,曼联!

A Contest to Find Ads Worth Passing on / 058
竞赛——寻找值得传播的广告

Get Your Ph.D. in Lady Gaga / 064
重新认识女神嘎嘎

The Reality Principle / 070
真实原则

Did Mark Zuckerberg's Inspiration for Facebook Come Before Harvard? / 076
马克·扎克伯格的灵感源头

In a Battle of the E-Readers, Booksellers Spurn Superheroes / 083
电子读者的争夺战，超级英雄的牺牲地

Michael Jordan's 10 Secrets to Reaching the Top / 090
迈克尔·乔丹攀上巅峰的十大秘诀

How to Live Before You Die / 099
我生未竟，精彩不断

I Think（and Write in a Journal），Therefore I Am / 105
我思、我写，故我在

They Teach Happiness at Harvard / 110
哈佛的幸福人生

Burning Man：Puts Other Festivals in the Shade / 116
妙趣横生——火人节

Learning to Brake for Butterflies / 122
停车赏蝶

Beauty：When the Other Dancer Is the Self / 128
美：当另一位舞者是自己

Unlocking the Secrets of French Women / 136
掀开她们的面纱

Why Pink Doesn't Stink / 142
粉色可不恶心

Crazy Over Crosswords / 148
黑白之恋

SUVs：Killer Cars / 155
杀手汽车

Europeans Just Want to Have Fun / 161
及时行乐在欧洲

Keeping Up With Coffee Culture / 167
咖啡文化寻源

An English Girl in Paris / 173
英国女孩的巴黎之旅

Death in the Afternoon：Hemingway Now Writes of Bull-Fighting as an Art / 178
《午后之死》——海明威与斗牛艺术

Hidden Within Technology's Empire, a Republic of Letters / 185
隐匿于技术帝国中的一方文学理想国

透 视 PERCEPTION

Reading Guidance

手机从不离身,哪怕是上厕所;工作、购物、交流基本依靠电脑和手机解决;除了工作、休息和吃饭,大部分时间都泡在网上……这可能是很多人生活的真实写照。如今,电脑和手机已经成为我们生活、工作必不可少的工具,拉近了人与人的距离,我们已经不能想象,如果没有手机和电脑,生活会变成什么样。有人在网上发表感慨"没有手机和电脑我想我们的生活会一塌糊涂,两眼迷茫,三餐无味,四面楚歌,五心不定,六神无主,七零八落……久而久之,实在难熬,百般无奈,千呼万唤,万万使不得"。情况真的是这样吗? 阅读本文,你一定会从中了解另一种态度。

Shakespeare Had No BlackBerry and Aristotle Managed Without an iPhone

Putting down some of our hi-tech gadgets and hi-octane pastimes might help us make a lot less impact…

I've often said that far more sensible than a "make poverty history" campaign would be a "make wealth history" campaign. It is, after all, the wealthy people who do all the damage. The less money you earn, the fewer resources you use up.

〈001〉

I am not for a second recommending a worldwide "wealth relief" policy, where we will steal money from the rich and give it to the poor, though that idea certainly has its attractions.

However, it makes perfect rational sense to argue that the planet could be healed if we all lived more modestly. All of our technology is completely unnecessary to a happy life. Westernizing the world by commodifying everything, will have the effect of increasing demand for oil, when everyone knows that the sensible thing is to reduce demand.

Fred Pearce of the *New Scientist* has expressed this idea in terms of carbon emissions:

The world's richest half billion people—that's about seven per cent of the global population—are responsible for fifty per cent of the world's emissions. Meanwhile, the poorest fifty per cent are responsible for just seven per cent of emissions. One American or European is more often than not responsible for more emissions than an entire village of Africans.

It's pretty obvious that Western lifestyles which rely on gigantic amounts of electricity use up far more resources than a subsistence-based life. A little more poverty would be a good thing. The recession itself, in fact, has already slowed down carbon emissions. The International Energy Agency says in a recent report that emissions are likely to fall by 3 per cent in 2009 as a direct result of the recession.

Our addiction to computers is one of the problems. It is curious that the computer has become an almost indispensable piece of equipment, even for the most determined downshifter. Today's Thoreau might be able to turn his back on many elements of industrial capitalism, but he will not do without his laptop and his Google connection. A seriously green campaigner would give up his or her mobile phone and computer because both are made of plastic and are destined to end up in the rubbish bin.

We did actually manage quite well for many millennia without computers or

透视 PERCEPTION

mobile phones. Shakespeare had no BlackBerry; Aristotle managed without an iPhone. Christ preached his sermon on the mount without the need of a PA system and Powerpoint presentation. All of our technology is completely unnecessary to a happy life.

We should have one day where we turn off the computers and the machines and let them rest. For ourselves, we should eat and walk and drink. We should stay at home. If we lived poor for just one day of the week, we would instantly reduce pollution by a seventh. We would rediscover the simple pleasures, such as cards, chess, backgammon, draughts, talking, dancing and playing music. We would create our own pleasures rather than parting with our hard-earned cash to receive entertainments created by other people. Can we live as happy peasants, creative, fulfilled, in touch with the land? I see *Sundays* along the lines of the following extract from a 1949 essay called *Portrait of a Parish*, written by Essex farmer's wife Ethelind Fearon:

We do not suffer ourselves to be amused, sitting inert before a screen or watching dogs and horses and busy men with wind-filled balls running for our entertainment. If there is running to be done we will do it. We make our own amusements, our own clothes from our own sheep's wool dyed from our own walnut trees, our own cakes and jams and toys and rugs, gloves, sheepskin slippers, cricket bats, bricks, baskets, beehives, and our own beautiful farm wagons from local trees.

Such a life is not an absurd fantasy, a silly romantic dream. It is a perfectly sensible way of doing things.

Notes

gigantic：巨大的
backgammon：西洋双陆棋
walnut：胡桃

莎翁没有"黑莓"，
亚里士多德也没有"苹果"

放下一些我们手里的高科技玩意儿，放弃高能耗的娱乐方式，或许会对地球造成较小的影响……

我经常说，比起"让贫困成为历史"的活动，"让富有成为历史"更为合理。毕竟，破坏都是富人们造成的。你赚的钱越少，消耗的资源也就越少。

我完全不是在推荐全球范围的"财富救济"政策，即劫富济贫，虽然这个想法相当有吸引力。我们也必须记得，穷困潦倒没有任何吸引人的地方。

然而，我们有理由相信，如果我们生活得更加节俭，是有可能拯救地球的。我们所有的科技对于幸福生活来说完全没有必要。将一切事物商品化从而使整个世界走西方道路，会导致石油需求增大，而每个人都知道减少需求才是明智的选择。

《新科学家》杂志社的弗莱德·皮尔斯从碳排放的角度阐明了以上观点：世界上最富有的5亿人——约占全球总人口的7%——碳排放量占了全球总量的一半。然而，最贫穷的50%人口的碳排放量只占碳排放总量的7%。一个美国人或一个欧洲人常常比非洲一个村庄的碳排放量还多。

很明显，依赖于巨大电力的西方生活方式与单纯以维持生命为目的的生活方式相比，资源消耗量要高出许多。稍微穷一点或许是件好事。事实上，经济衰退已经使碳排放量降低。国际能源机构在近期一份报告中表示，由于受经济衰退的直接影响，2009年的碳排放量可能降低3%。

我们对于电脑的依赖也是一个问题。令人惊奇的是电脑几乎成了一个不可或缺的工具，即便对那些追求简单生活的人来说也是这样。即便是梭罗(19世纪美国最具世界影响力的作家、哲学家,他的思想激励了那些寻求返璞归真的人)生活在现代,他或许会对工业资本主义的众多元素嗤之以鼻,但他很难放弃笔记本电脑和谷歌连接。一个非常严肃的环保倡导者才可能会放弃他(她)的手机和电脑,因为二者都是塑料制品,最终难逃被丢弃到垃圾桶的命运。

在过去几千年没有电脑和手机的日子里我们都过得不错。莎士比亚没有"黑莓",亚里士多德没有"苹果"。耶稣在山上训诫时也没使用广播系统或用幻灯做展示。所有的科技对于幸福生活来说完全没有必要。

我们应该选择一天关上电脑和各种机器,让它们休息。我们自己则吃饭,散步,喝酒,待在家里。如果一周过一天贫穷的生活,污染会立刻减少七分之一。我们会重新发现简单的乐趣,比如打牌、国际象棋、西洋双陆棋、跳棋、聊天、跳舞,还有演奏音乐。我们可以自娱自乐,而不用花辛苦赚到的钱购买别人提供的各种娱乐方式。我们能不能像农民那样快乐生活,有所创造,充实满足,亲近自然?我在《周日》杂志上看到这样一段话,出自一篇发表于1949年的文章《牧区的风貌》,作者是埃塞克斯的一名农妇费伦:"我们无须为了获得娱乐而劳心费神,比如一动不动地坐在电视前,或者看着马儿、狗儿,抑或看着忙碌的人们带着充气皮球四处奔跑讨我们欢心。如果需要跑步,我们自己去跑。我们自己寻找快乐,自己做衣服,衣料就是自家饲养的绵羊的毛皮,还用自己种的胡桃树染色。我们自己做蛋糕、果酱、玩具、小毯子、手套、羊皮拖鞋、板球拍、砖块、篮子、蜂房,还用本地树木做一架漂亮的农场马车。"

这种生活并不是荒唐的幻想或愚蠢的浪漫梦境。这是极为明智的处事之道。

More to Read

　　怎样做到低碳生活？本文作者给出的建议是远离高科技产品，生活节俭甚至贫穷。这显然是一个反技术主义者的论调，虽然稍显偏激，但不无道理。人类总在扩展自己的欲望，渴望拥有更快的速度，更广阔的视野，更多的资讯，更丰富的物质生活。但我们是不是也要停下脚步想一想：我们要的到底是什么？高科技带给我们的又是什么？

透视 PERCEPTION

Reading Guidance

2009年6月26日,流行音乐之王迈克尔·杰克逊突然告别了这个世界,我们终于意识到自己失去了什么。曾经的辉煌和质疑变成铺天盖地的纪念和致敬,数以百万计的粉丝向流行歌曲天王道别。而人们能够了解这个舞台之神么?他是音乐史上最畅销的流行歌手,也是世界上拥有最多歌迷的歌手,他为慈善事业捐款3亿美元,是全世界以个人名义捐助慈善事业最多的艺人,独自支持了世界上39个慈善救助基金会。但不幸的是,他也是一个被媒体污蔑最多、被世人误解最深的人。或许杰克逊最想做的事情只是坐在梦幻庄园(neverland)那棵大树上,向往和小飞侠彼得·潘一样不要长大……本文作为杰克逊的纪念文章,独辟蹊径,以他的舞蹈为切入点,回顾了这位流行音乐之王的成长之路。

Walking on the Moon—Michael Jackson in Motion

If you watch a video of the Jackson 5 performing *I Want You Back*, on the Ed Sullivan show, in 1969, you will see that the group's lead vocalist—Michael, the youngest of the five brothers—was already an A-list dancer at the age of eleven. Here is this fat-cheeked boy, in a pink hat that he is obviously proud

of, doing tilts and dips and fanny rocks and finger snaps, and tucking in little extras—half steps, quarter steps—between them. Most amazing is his musicality, his ability to respond to the score faithfully and yet creatively, playing with the music, moving in before and after the beat. Musicality always comes off as spontaneity, and he was loved, early on, for that quality.

Now turn to *Don't Stop 'Til You Get Enough* (1979). Ten years have passed. He has started recording his own songs. He does fancier steps. But at twenty-one, as at eleven, he is galvanizing above all because of his naturalness. He hops with joy; he wags his head; his shirt comes untucked.

Then come the landmark videos of the early nineteen-eighties: *Billie Jean*, *Beat It*, and *Thriller*, all of them for songs that appeared on the collection *Thriller* (1982), which is the best-selling album of all time. At this point, Jackson has just about everything you would want in a dancer. He is very fast, and, now that the adult musculature has come in, his whole body is "worked". As a result, he has a sharp attack, and wonderful clarity. Watch him—as you can, for example, in *The Way You Make Me Feel* (1987)—dancing, silhouetted, alongside other men doing the same steps. You can't see the faces, but you know which one he is. He dives into a step more intently, and shows it to us more precisely, than anyone else. Around this time, the videos are featuring some new moves—for example, multiple spins. And he's now doing the famous moonwalk, which he picked up from break dancing.

The *Thriller*-period videos were instrumental in converting MTV from a backwater to a sensation. Jackson consciously aimed at doing that. "I wanted to be a pioneer in this relatively new medium," he said in his 1988 memoir, *Moon Walk*. He spent a fortune on these projects. The 1995 *Scream* video cost seven million dollars—a record at that time. He didn't like to call these works videos. They were "short films," he claimed—and rightly, for he had them shot not on videotape but on 35mm film. "We were serious," he said.

Jackson took his choreography from a number of sources: hip-hop, sock hop, disco, and jazz dance, plus a little tap and Charleston. By his account, he constructed some of the movement himself. *Billie Jean*, he says in *Moon Walk*, still had no dance component the night before he was scheduled to perform it in honor of Motown's twenty-fifth anniversary. He went down to the kitchen, turned on the music full blast, and, in his words, "let the dance create itself" on his body. His moonwalk had its début in that number.

But on most of his dances he did not work alone. Many experienced stage and TV choreographers collaborated with Jackson. On the PBS special *Everybody Dance Now* (1991), in answer to a question from the dance historian, Michael Peters said that Jackson's method was to put together some steps and ideas and bring them to a choreographer, who would then organize them into a coherent dance.

Pop critics often say that with the *Thriller* album, though it came early — he was only twenty-four—Jackson went as far as he ever got musically. The same might be said of the music videos born of this album. The *Thriller* video became part of world culture. On YouTube, you can see a clip of fifteen hundred inmates of a Detention and Rehabilitation Center, in the Philippines, doing the *Thriller* dance in unison, in their orange uniforms. (Prison officials thought it would be a good lesson in discipline.) The later videos were not as popular, because they were not as good. Now, in place of dancing and stories, he ramped up the pyrotechnics. Smoke banks enclose him. Great flames shoot up behind him. (Back in 1984, while he was filming a Pepsi commercial, the special effects set his hair on fire. He had to be treated for third-degree burns.)

The last known video shows him at a rehearsal for the London season he was about to embark on. He struts, he boogies; he snaps and pops. As CNN's chief medical correspondent, Sanjay Gupta, said, "This doesn't look like someone who's very sick to me." That's not to mention that Jackson was fifty years old and, because he was in rehearsal, was probably not performing "full out".

He was still a great dancer. Two days later, he was dead.

Notes

spontaneity：自然流露
galvanize：激励
silhouette：剪影，轮廓
choreography：编舞者
inmate：囚犯

月球漫步——舞动的迈克尔·杰克逊

　　如果你看看"杰克逊五人"乐队1969年在爱德·沙利文演出《我要你回来》的录像，就会发现乐队的领唱——迈克尔——五兄弟中最小的那个，已经是一个一流的舞者了，虽然他当时只有11岁。这个脸颊胖嘟嘟的小男孩，带着他引以为豪的粉色帽子，做着各种动作——倾斜、俯身，扭着屁股，打着响指，还时不时地加进一些特别动作——半步、四分之一步。最令人惊奇的是他的乐感，他能恰到好处又不失创意地对乐曲做出反应，随音乐舞动，在节拍前后，音乐的律动在他身上即兴散发。也正因为此，他受到大家喜爱。

　　十年荏苒，杰克逊已经开始录制自己的歌曲了——《直到你满足为止》（1979）——此时，他的舞步更加精彩。21岁的他乐感亦如11岁的时候，自然随性的音乐天赋使他独占鳌头。他欢快地舞动，左右摆头，衬衫散在腰间。

透视 PERCEPTION

再来看看他 20 世纪 80 年代早期具有标志性的音乐录影带,《比利·珍》、《打击》、《颤栗者》,这些歌都出自有史以来最畅销的唱片《颤栗者》。此时的杰克逊已经具有一个优秀舞者的全部素质了。这时的他舞步敏捷,成年人的肌肉系统已经开始显现,整个身体被"激活"了。他的舞步非常锋利强劲,干净利落。比如,在《你给我的感觉》(1987)里,他现出的只是剪影,与其他伴舞一起跳着同样的舞步。虽然看不到他的脸,但是你知道哪个是杰克逊。他比其他人跳得更专注,舞步也更精准。在这个时期杰克逊的音乐录影带中总能看到一些新的舞蹈动作,比如多圈旋转,此时,他已经在跳著名的月球漫步了,那是他从霹雳舞里吸收进来的舞步。

《颤栗者》时期的音乐录影带帮助"MTV"从停滞萎靡的状态成为轰动一时的文艺形式。杰克逊有意为之。他在 1988 年的回忆录《月球漫步》里写道:"我想要成为这种新的艺术媒介的先行者。"他在这些项目上花费了巨资。1995 年的《惊声尖叫》耗资 700 万美元——创下了当时的纪录。他不愿把这些作品称为录影,他主张应该叫做"短篇电影"——的确如此,因为这些作品不是用录像带录制的,而是用 35 毫米的胶片拍摄的。"我们是严肃的,"他说。

杰克逊的舞蹈艺术吸收了各种风格:嘻哈、短袜舞、迪斯科、爵士舞,还有一点踢踏舞和查尔斯顿舞。按照他的说法,他还原创了一些动作。迈克尔在《月球漫步》里回忆道,就在参加摩城唱片公司 25 周年晚会的前一天晚上,《比利·珍》的舞蹈仍然没有编好。他下楼到厨房,把音响开到最大,让舞蹈在身体上"自己创造出来"。"月球漫步"的舞步在这首歌里第一次出现。

但事实上多数编舞不是他独自完成的。很多经验丰富的舞台和电视编舞者都与杰克逊合作过。1991 年,在美国公共广播公司(PBS)的特别节目《大家来跳舞》中,迈克尔·皮特斯在回答一位舞蹈史学家的问题时说,杰克逊经常采用的方法就是把舞步和创意集收集到一起,然后把它们交给一个编舞者,由这个编舞者来组织成连贯的舞蹈。

流行乐评论家常说,《颤栗者》专辑虽然很早问世——杰克逊当时只有 24 岁——却是杰克逊的巅峰之作。这张专辑的音乐录影得到同样的评价。

〈011〉

《颤栗者》已经成为世界文化的一部分。在"YouTube"上,你能找到一段影片:菲律宾一个拘留感化院里,1500名犯人穿着橘红色的囚服同跳"颤栗者"(狱方认为这有助于加强纪律管理)。杰克逊后期的音乐录影作品由于水准良莠不齐就没那么流行了。与舞蹈、情节相比,杰克逊变得更重视烟火效果。烟火总是包围着他,烈焰从他身后腾起。(1984年,拍百事可乐广告时,烟火特效烧着了他的头发,他因三级烧伤不得不住院治疗。)后来他又迷上了电脑特技——突然消失,突然出现,在墙上行走。

人们看到杰克逊的最后录影是他为伦敦演唱会进行的排练。他昂首阔步,跳霹雳舞,动作敏捷。美国有线新闻网(CNN)的首席医学记者山泽古普塔说:"我看不出他是一个病得很严重的人。"更不用说杰克逊已经50岁了,而且因为是排练,他可能并没有使出全部力气——他仍然是一个伟大的舞者。两天后,迈克尔·杰克逊辞世了。

More to Read

"月球漫步"也称为"太空漫步"或"滑步",迈克尔·杰克逊在《比利·珍》的表演中第一次使用就即刻引起轰动,并成为他招牌动作之一。这种舞蹈动作会使舞蹈者看起来像是往前迈步,实际上却向后移动。不过对于迈克尔·杰克逊来说,"月球漫步"不仅仅是媒体为他的舞步起的名字。杰克逊自己投资拍摄的音乐电影名字就叫《月球漫步》。在这部电影中,他一身短小的西装,一顶压得很低的礼帽,袖子上扎着一个袖标,所有这些都成为了杰克逊个人神话中不可替代的标志性符号。在1988年,迈克尔·杰克逊出版自传《月球漫步》,书中说道:"大家说如果我继续离群索居,最后可能落得和他(猫王)一样的死法。我对于猫王如何走向自我毁灭很有兴趣,但不想和他走相同的路。"猫王因服药过量在家中暴毙,年仅42岁。然而杰克逊因心跳停止猝死,人生同样在壮年时谢幕。

透视 PERCEPTION

Reading Guidance

美国动画大致可分成两类：一是主流动画，大家熟悉的迪斯尼、梦工厂不必多说，一个是炮制合家欢童话的高手，一个是打造大团圆结局的专家，制作的动画也都是老少咸宜，不分国界。二是另类一派，以强烈的个性和独特的视角赢得掌声，本文谈到的动画片《南方公园》正是这一派中的佼佼者。《南方公园》用夸张手法讲述深刻主题，不仅仅是恶搞，更是对热门话题、明星名人的讽刺解构。因此，《南方公园》并不是拍给儿童看的轻松的小品，而是拍给成人看的，集讽刺之能事的大作。1997年，《南方公园》在美国刚一播放，就约有540万人观看，人气之旺出乎所有人的意料。之后《南方公园》不仅创下了美国喜剧中心频道（Comedy Central）有史以来最高收视率纪录，更被《纽约时报》等媒体评为1997年10大最佳电视节目，入围多项电视相关奖项。然而创出如此佳绩的动画系列片的幕后主创是谁？他们如何在十几年的时间里合作并获得成功？不妨读一读下面这篇文章。

South Park Has a Silent Partner

There are many different jobs a writer can get in the television industry, but the most fun of all is a job where you don't really have to work. Is Matt Stone, co-creator of the cartoon *South Park*, doing a job like that? Or can he be

an equal partner on his show without actually writing it?

Stone and Trey Parker are both listed as executive producers of *South Park*, and they appear jointly for most interviews about the show. But Stone hasn't been credited with writing an episode in years. For the last eight seasons, Parker has written every episode, with Stone and a few staff writers contributing ideas but not full scripts. Parker now directs every episode as well. Most of the regular and guest characters are voiced by Parker, though Stone still handles the voices he did in the original pilot, Kyle and Kenny (who no longer gets killed every week). So while Matt Stone is still the "executive producer", does he do much to earn that title?

Some fans insist that he doesn't. Mocking Stone is a regular pastime among people who discuss *South Park* on message boards; a typical posting reads: "Trey writes every episode and then does the majority of the voices and most of the music while Matt sits around and laughs at Trey to encourage him." And it's obviously true that Parker is responsible for *South Park* as the crude, foul-mouthed work of art it is, and Stone really isn't. But producing a TV series entails more than just the artistry. That's where Stone comes in.

While Parker is handling the creative side of the show, someone needs to pull together the other elements of production. That's particularly true on a show like *South Park*, where episodes are routinely written and produced only a few days before they air. So while Stone occasionally directed episodes in the early years of the show, he's found his niche as the person who coordinates the episodes, making sure they arrive on time and under budget. This is the business side of things, which Parker can't handle because he's too busy writing and directing. Stone has no problem with focusing on his producing duties; he said that "I am not a good director, I know that. I am not a very good actor either, and I know it, but it is good to know that."

Another important job Stone appears to have is as Parker's minder, his show-business babysitter. Like a lot of talented writers, Parker is self-admittedly anti-social, and prefers to stay home and work rather than deal with conflict. So Stone does it for him.

And he can keep Parker from doing in life what he does in his scripts. As a writer and as a person, Parker likes to say outrageous things to get a rise out of people. Once at a party, Parker went up to a woman and proclaimed "George Bush is a great man" just to make her angry. Without Stone to act as a go-between, you can imagine how Parker might say something just to get a network executive angry. Every artist needs someone to protect him from himself.

And, finally, Stone has an important but annoying job: dealing with the media. When an episode sparks the controversy that Parker clearly craves—like this year's episode where the Queen of England commits suicide—Stone gives the interviews explaining that it's all in fun. And when voice actor Isaac Hayes quit the show last year over its attack on Scientology, it was Stone who went to the press and remarked that Hayes "got a sudden case of religious sensitivity when it was his religion featured on the show". Without Stone to defuse the controversy, Parker might not be able to get away with offending everyone all the time.

Without Parker, *South Park* would never get written, but without Stone, the episodes would never get made. In making a good television show, there are more important things than creativity.

Notes

entail:需要
niche:合适的工作
crave:渴望

《南方公园》那位沉默的合伙人

　　电视产业里，作家可以得到很多不同的工作，但其中最有趣的一种是你其实不需要工作。马特·斯通——卡通片《南方公园》的合伙创建人，是否正在做这样一份工作呢？或者他虽然没有写作，但仍是这个节目重要的合作者？

　　斯通和崔伊·帕克同被列为《南方公园》的执行制片人，而且他们经常同时出现在关于此节目的访谈中。但是，几年来斯通没有写过任何一集。在过去的八季里，帕克编写了每一集节目，斯通和其他几位撰稿人提供想法但不编台词。并且现在帕克还导演每一集节目。大多数的常规和客串角色都由帕克配音，虽然斯通仍在负责他在最初的样片里配音的角色——凯乐和肯尼（他不再每周都被杀了）。那么，尽管马特·斯通仍然是"执行制片"，他真的配得上这个头衔吗？

　　一些粉丝坚持认为他没有。在《南方公园》留言板上，拿斯通开玩笑是讨论者们的一大消遣，典型的帖子是这样的："崔伊为每一集编剧，然后完成绝大多数的配音和配乐，而马特到处闲坐，取笑崔伊，以此来鼓励他。"很明显，让《南方公园》成为现在这样自然原味、"粗口"成章的艺术作品的，的确是帕克而并非斯通。然而制作一部电视节目需要的不只是艺术。这就是斯通擅长的地方。

　　当帕克负责节目的创意方面时，需要有人来把制作中的其他元素组织起来。对于像《南方公园》这样的节目而言更是如此，因为每一集都几乎是在播出的前几天才制作好。所以，虽然在节目刚起步的时候斯通也曾偶尔导演几集，但他发现自己更擅长统筹管理，确保能按时按预算完成片子。

帕克因为要忙于编剧和导演，而无法顾及这些商业层面的事情。斯通非常清楚自己的职责所在。他说："我不是一个好导演，我很清楚。我不是一个好演员，我也很清楚，但对自己有清楚的了解是件好事。"

斯通的另外一项重要工作是照顾帕克，当他电视事业里的保姆。与许多有才华的作家一样，帕克自认为反社会，他喜欢待在家里工作，不愿处理各种冲突矛盾。于是，斯通包办了那些令帕克头痛的事情。

同时，斯通还可以防止帕克把剧本里表现出的作风带到现实中去。不论是作为一个编剧，还是一个普通人，帕克都喜欢说些骇人的话来捉弄或者激怒别人。帕克曾在一个聚会上特意走到一位女士旁边对她说："乔治·布什是个伟人。"目的只是为了惹那位女士生气。没有斯通做中间人的话，你可以想象帕克可能为了激怒网站主管而冒出怎样的言辞。每一位艺术家都需要一个保护者，以避免自我伤害。

最后，斯通还有一项重要但令人生厌的工作——应付媒体。如果一集节目如帕克所愿激起了广泛争议（比如今年英女皇自杀的那集），斯通会出面接受采访，解释这些仅是出于娱乐目的。为人物配音的艾萨克·海耶斯辞演，理由是一集节目攻击了他所信仰的基督教科学派，也是斯通出来面对媒体，评价海耶斯"因为自己的信仰出现在节目中而突然变得宗教敏感了"。如果没有斯通来平息争议，帕克就无法一边不断地激怒所有人，一边安然无恙。

没有帕克，《南方公园》就不会被创作出来，而没有斯通，剧集恐怕永远无法被制作播出。在一部优秀电视节目的制作过程中，有一些事情比创意更重要。

More to Read

　　本文围绕两位主创者的分工而展开话题，使读者在了解《南方公园》一些幕后的制作故事的同时，也对两位个性张扬的创作者有所认识。其实《南方公园》里那四个圆头圆脑的小男孩中，有两个正是这两位创作者的化身：认真、敏感的斯坦是帕克的化身，而持怀疑主义的犹太孩子凯勒是斯通的化身。斯通和帕克，一个是创意天才，一个是有全局观的思想者，他们二人珠联璧合，共同打造了美国历史上最流行、最疯狂、最具争议的动画片。

透 视 PERCEPTION

Reading Guidance

　　奥普拉·温芙蕾是当今世界上最具影响力的女性之一。自1986年以她的名字命名的脱口秀节目在全美推出以来,她幽默、机智、真诚、自然的风格便迅速捕获了无数美国观众的心。如今,她以超过23亿美元的身家在美国黑人亿万富翁中名列第一;她在近8年里连续5次被评为全美最受欢迎主持人;她在电视读书会节目中推荐过的新书转眼就会成为畅销书;美国伊利诺伊大学开设了一门课程专门研究这种以奥普拉为标志的"美国文化现象";她在斯皮尔伯格的电影《紫色》中出演角色,荣获了当年奥斯卡最佳女配角的提名;作为亿万富婆的她同样没忘记回馈社会,她通过自己设立的慈善机构向贫困妇女、儿童和家庭伸出援助之手。然而,这位传媒女皇并没有满足于自己所取得的成就,她还要更大的舞台。本文以奥普拉停播自己的脱口秀节目,转而开办全新的有线电视台为话题,着重分析奥普拉对于自身品牌的打造与传播,如何从一档成功的电视节目步步升级为涉及多个领域的传媒帝国,而新频道的开播既是奥普拉品牌更大的平台,也是她不断挑战自我的体现。奥普拉以自己的智慧、善良、勤奋为大家树立了榜样。

Brand Loyalty

It was one of the most tear-stained moments in the 26-year history of a

show that specializes in tear-stained moments. Oprah Winfrey announced that she will end her eponymous show in September, 2011. She loves her show enough to know when it is time to say goodbye, she told her traumatized audience.

The sound of crying could be heard from sea to shining sea. For once the pundits sang the same song as "real Americans". They talked breathlessly about Ms. Winfrey's up-from-the-bootstraps achievements—how she came from nothing to amass a fortune of $2.3 billion and how she has viewers in more than 100 countries—and pronounced her retirement the end of an era.

The only problem with all this commentary is that Ms. Winfrey is not quitting. She is ending her relationship with a big network, CBS, in order to devote herself to an ambitious new venture, a cable-television channel to be called the Oprah Winfrey Network, or OWN, which she plans to launch in January 2011 as a joint-venture with Discovery Communications. The world is about to be blessed with more Oprah, rather than less.

This is a tricky transition that raises all sorts of questions about the power of personal brands. Martha Stewart, who was once the nearest equivalent to Ms. Winfrey, had started to devalue her brand even before she got into trouble with the law, spreading herself too thin and striking too many deals with retailers. *The Oprah Winfrey Show* is not just a "delivery channel" that she can close down at will: it has defined its creator for 26 years. By killing off her brand-creating show and diluting her personal contribution across an entire network, she runs the risk of enraging her fans.

But there are good commercial reasons for Ms. Winfrey's decision. The audience for network television has been declining relentlessly as viewers have migrated to cable and the internet. The audience for *The Oprah Winfrey Show* has shrunk from about 14m viewers in 1998 to about 7m today, though it still remains the highest-rated talk show. Ms. Winfrey is simply following her audience into a more fragmented media world. Besides, there is nothing to stop Ms. Winfrey reviving *The Oprah Winfrey Show*, or something very like it, on her new platform.

Ms. Winfrey also has lots of experiences at relaunching herself. She reinvented the daytime talk show not once but twice—first by exposing some of her innermost secrets in public (about how she was raped at the age of nine and experimented with drugs in her 20s, for example) and second by taking her show upmarket.

Ms. Winfrey is also an experienced brand-stretcher. She has starred in a number of successful films, most notably *The Color Purple*, for which she was nominated for an Oscar; more importantly, **she h**as launched a succession of Oprah-related products such as her website, Oprah.com and her magazine, *O*. Each time she succeeded in extending her audience without alienating her most loyal fans: a year after *O*'s launch in 2000 half its readers were not regular watchers of *The Oprah Winfrey Show*, including many professional women who would never dream of watching television in the afternoon.

Ms. Winfrey has always been a vigilant steward of her brand. She is also notorious for her overbearing perfectionism. Ms. Winfrey has steadfastly refused to take her company public. She has also refused to strike deals with retailers or stick her name on merchandise, as numerous celebrity chefs and athletes have done.

Such vigilance about her brand is hardly a guarantee of success in the volatile and cacophonous media market. Her film version of Toni Morrison's *Beloved* earned only $23 million, less than half what it cost to make. Her earlier tentative venture into the cable market, with Oxygen Media, enjoyed limited success. But Ms. Winfrey's handful of failures are as nothing compared with her successes. Perhaps more than any of her rivals Ms. Winfrey understands that it is hard to fail in the media business if you put your faith in people's appetite for stories of those who pick themselves up from the floor and make something of their lives.

Notes

vigilant：警惕的，警觉的
volatile：动荡不定的
cacophonous：刺耳嘈杂的

品牌忠诚

这个专注于打动人心的节目至今（2009 年）已经播放了 24 年，现在到了它最催人泪下的时刻——奥普拉·温芙蕾宣布将于 2011 年 9 月结束她的同名脱口秀节目。奥普拉·温芙蕾告诉极度震惊的观众们，她热爱自己的节目，因此知道什么时候该说再见。

哭泣声从西海岸传到了东海岸。难得一次权威人士们唱着同样的论调，称赞奥普拉·温芙蕾是"真正的美国人"。他们交口称赞温芙蕾女士靠自身奋斗一步一步取得成就——她怎样从一无所有到聚集了 23 亿美元的财富，拥有 100 多个国家的观众——并宣告她的退役是一个时代的结束。

所有这些评论唯一的问题是，温芙蕾女士并非要离开。她要结束与大电视台哥伦比亚广播公司（CBS）的合作，为的是投身于一项抱负远大的新尝试，即开办名为奥普拉·温芙蕾电视网的有限电视频道，这是她和探索发现公司的合资项目，计划于 2011 年 1 月开播。世界即将有更多的奥普拉，而非更少。

这个微妙的转变引发了许多关于个人品牌力量的疑问。玛莎·斯图尔特曾经是与奥普拉平起平坐的成功人物，但在她惹上官司之前，她的品牌价值已经缩水。原因就是过分铺张自己的品牌，与众多零售商签订合同。《奥普拉·温芙蕾脱口秀》并不只是随奥普拉的意志就能关闭的"派送频道"——26年来,这档节目一直代表着它的创作者。奥普拉终断其招牌节目,将个人影响力稀释于整个电视网中,这么做是冒险的,很有可能激怒自己的粉丝。

但是温芙蕾女士的决定有良好的商业考量。由于有线电视和网络的兴起,电视台的观众在不断流失。尽管在脱口秀类节目中,《奥普拉·温芙蕾脱口秀》节目的收视率仍高居榜首,但观众人数从1998年的1400万缩减到如今的大约700万。温芙蕾女士只是跟上观众们的步伐,进入更加细分的媒体世界。而且,没有任何东西可以阻止奥普拉在她的新平台上复播《奥普拉·温芙蕾脱口秀》,或任何与之相似的节目。

温芙蕾女士也有很多重新推出自己的经验。她曾不止一次——确切地说是两次重新改版日间脱口秀,第一次是在公众面前坦露自己的一些内心秘密(例如有关她9岁时遭遇性侵犯,20多岁时曾经吸毒),第二次是将节目推向高端市场。

温芙蕾女士在品牌拓展方面也有丰富的经验。她出演了一系列成功的电影,最出名的是《紫色》,并以此片提名奥斯卡奖;更为重要的是,她推出了一系列奥普拉周边产品,诸如自己的网站(Oprah.com)、杂志(《O》)。每次动作都使她成功地扩展了自己的观众,而非疏远自己的铁杆粉丝。她的杂志于2000年发行,之后的一年时间,读者已经由《奥普拉·温芙蕾脱口秀》的固定观众拓展到很多从未想到自己会在下午看电视的职业女性。

温芙蕾女士一直对自己的品牌管理保持警醒。她也因其傲慢的完美主义而恶名远扬。温芙蕾女士坚决拒绝将自己的公司上市。她也拒绝与零售商达成交易,像许多名厨和运动员那样将自己的名字印在商品上。

然而这样的警惕、严谨也很难保证在动荡嘈杂的媒体市场取得成功。温芙蕾女士把托妮·莫里森的《被爱》搬上大荧幕,收入仅2300万美元,不及成本的一半。她早期曾尝试与氧气媒体合作进入有线电视市场,获得的成功也非常有限。但与奥普拉的巨大成就相比,寥寥几次失败微不足道。或许温芙蕾女士比她的任何一个竞争对手都明白,如果你的信念与观众的需求相吻合,讲述那些曾经跌倒,但努力爬起来并取得成功的人生经历,就

很难在传媒事业中失败。

More to Read

风光无限的背后往往是不为人知的寒苦,奥普拉的成功史就是这样一部传奇的励志片。她是女人,又是黑人,在成名前还是穷人;没有令人惊艳的外表,没有值得夸耀的家庭背景。相反,草根出身的她有着极其心酸的成长之路。少女奥普拉是典型的"问题少女",终日厮混、酗酒、抽烟、堕胎、自暴自弃。是父亲的管教和爱把奥普拉从沉沦的深渊中救起。对经历过不堪回首的童年、叛逆堕落的少女时代的奥普拉来说,她只是靠着"一个人可以非常清贫、困顿、低微,但是不可以没有梦想"的简单信念,实现了丑小鸭到黑天鹅的美丽蜕变。

透视 PERCEPTION

Reading Guidance

要问时下最火的小游戏是什么，那当然非《愤怒的小鸟》莫属了。这款开发成本只有10万美元的游戏，却成了十足的吸金王，让开发商罗维奥在赚足了人气的同时收获颇丰，不可谓不成功。《愤怒的小鸟》是罗维奥游戏公司的第52款游戏，而在推出这款游戏之前，该公司已经濒临破产的边缘。犹如当年坂口博信推出《最终幻想》游戏一样，《愤怒的小鸟》挽救了罗维奥游戏公司，也使其进入了高速发展阶段。"愤怒的小鸟"为什么能一飞冲天呢？本文作者从游戏设计本身，公司的创新商业模式，以及玩家的热捧等几个方面进行分析。了解到这些以后，或许当你再次打开这个游戏时，它就不再只是一个简单有趣的休闲游戏了。

Angry Birds, Flocking to Cellphones Everywhere

It sounds like a tough sell: a game that involves catapulting birds at elaborate fortresses constructed by evil pigs. But Angry Birds, a hit game by Rovio, a small Finnish company, is one of the unlikeliest pop-culture crazes of the year—and perhaps the first to make the leap from cellphone screens to the mainstream.

　　Angry Birds, in which the birds seek revenge on the egg-stealing pigs, is meant to be easily played in the checkout line and during other short windows of downtime—but some players have trouble stopping. Rovio says people around the world rack up 200 million minutes of game play each day.

　　Games like Angry Birds are reaching a wide audience of players who might never consider buying an Xbox or PlayStation, but are now carrying sophisticated game machines in their pockets—smartphones. Software developers, eager to become the next Rovio, are creating so-called casual games for this crowd, games that are easy to learn and hard to stop playing.

　　The trajectory of Angry Birds also suggests a larger shift in entertainment and in the kinds of brands that can win wide popularity. And unlike many of the best-known console video games—like the classic Super Mario Bros from Nintendo or the latest in the Call of Duty series, from Activision—cellphone games like Angry Birds are often made by small companies and catch on by word of mouth.

　　"There's no more formula," said James L. McQuivey, an analyst at Forrester Research who studies digital entertainment. "It doesn't matter where it starts: a ringtone, a video game, book. It has a shot at the big time."

　　On cellphones, he added, "anyone with coding skills, an idea and good characters can catch on without having to spend $100 million on a movie and marketing."

　　Jordan Finley, 30, who works at a legal consulting firm in Los Angeles, said he and his friend were such big fans of the game that they decided to create full-body bird costumes for Halloween.

　　"It was crazy," Mr. Finley said. "The people who didn't recognize it didn't understand, but people who knew the game loved it. Everyone wanted to take pictures. It felt like being chased by the paparazzi or something."

　　Fans of the game took to the streets on Saturday for Angry Birds Day, celebrating its first anniversary. Rovio worked with the Web service Meetup.com to help organize the gatherings in New York, London, Jakarta, Budapest and dozens of other cities, but fans stepped up to lead the gatherings. Rovio says it will create Angry Birds levels for the top 10 cities that celebrate Angry Birds Day.

Although Rovio has released two dozen other mobile games, none have come close to the success of Angry Birds, which cost about $100,000 to make and has been downloaded 50 million times in the last year. The paid version for the iPhone, which costs 99 cents in the United States, has brought in more than $8 million in revenue; Apple said last week that it was the best-selling iPhone app of 2010. The free version for phones running Google's Android software should produce $1 million a month in advertising revenue by the end of the year, Rovio says.

Peter Vesterbacka, Rovio's head of business development in North America, said the game was born when a Rovio designer sketched a rough outline of a bright red bird with a furious expression. "We didn't know what the game concept would be, but we loved the birds," he said. "The entire game and storyline was built around the birds."

Mr. Vesterbacka said the company took notice of the intricate storylines in Pixar films and the popularity of Mario. The stars of Angry Birds do not express themselves much apart from squawks and grunts, but players seem to be connecting with them all the same. "When thousands of people start dressing up as your characters, you know you're onto something," Mr. Vesterbacka said.

Rovio is trying to capitalize on its hit and is working on versions of Angry Birds for gaming consoles and PCs, along with a line of stuffed birds and pigs. It also hopes to spin the franchise into a movie or children's TV show.

"Rovio made a smart choice in making the birds angry," said Jesse Schell, a professor at Carnegie Mellon who studies game design and entertainment technology. "You can smash them into things and it's OK," he said. "Imagine if they were cute little birds. It might be kind of funny on some level, but most people would probably be a little repulsed."

Notes

trajectory：轨迹
repulse：拒绝接受

愤怒的小鸟，蜂拥飞至各地手机

　　用弹射的小鸟破坏邪恶猪建造的坚固城堡，这个游戏听起来似乎没什么销路。但事实却是，《愤怒的小鸟》这款由芬兰小公司——罗维奥游戏公司打造的手机游戏俨然成了当年最令人意想不到的热门游戏，它也将成为第一款从手机屏幕走向主流市场的游戏。

　　《愤怒的小鸟》是关于小鸟们向偷鸟蛋的猪发起报复的故事，游戏极易上手，结账排队或电脑死机时拿来短暂消磨时间非常不错，但有些玩家一上手就怎么都停不下来。据罗维奥公司称，每天全球玩家要花两亿分钟在这款游戏上。

　　《愤怒的小鸟》这类游戏将玩家群拓展到了那些永远不会购买微软游戏机（Xbox）或电视游戏机（Playstation）的人群当中，他们现在也随身携带自己先进的游戏机——智能电话。软件开发商们都渴望成为下一个罗维奥，他们正在为这一客户群开发所谓的休闲游戏。这种游戏上手简单，让人爱不释手。

　　《愤怒的小鸟》的发展轨迹也暗示了娱乐工业和品牌世界的巨大转变，任何人都可能赢得广泛的欢迎。不像以前那些视频游戏，例如任天堂的"超级玛丽"系列或美国动视的"使命召唤"系列，《愤怒的小鸟》这样的手机游戏往往出自小公司之手,依靠玩家口口相传。

弗雷斯特研究公司数字娱乐研究分析师詹姆斯·L.麦奎维就表示:"现在没有什么准则,英雄不问出处,手机铃声、视频游戏、书籍……任何人都可以取得成功。"说到手机,麦奎维表示:"只要你有编程技巧、出色的创意和角色设计就可以成功,而不需要花费1亿美元在宣传和营销上。"

今年30岁的乔丹·芬利在洛杉矶一家法律咨询公司工作,他说他和朋友是这个游戏的狂热粉丝,并决定为万圣节打造一套连身的愤怒小鸟装。他说:"这是个疯狂的主意,不认识小鸟的人无法理解,但玩过游戏的人都超喜欢。每个人都想来合影,感觉就像被狗仔队什么的围攻。"

《愤怒的小鸟》的玩家们周六还上街庆祝"愤怒小鸟日",祝贺游戏发行一周年。罗维奥公司与"Meetup"网站合作,组织在纽约、伦敦、雅加达、布达佩斯和其他城市的玩家活动,但上街聚集完全是玩家们自发的。罗维奥公司表示,他们还会评选出"愤怒小鸟日"的庆祝活动办得最有创意的十大城市。

虽然罗维奥公司还发布了其他24款手机游戏,但都没有《愤怒的小鸟》这么成功,《愤怒的小鸟》的开发成本只有10万美元,去年的下载数量就达到了5000万次。在美国,"iPhone"付费版的《愤怒的小鸟》定价99美分,目前已经带来超过800万美元的收入;苹果公司上周表示,《愤怒的小鸟》是2010年"iPhone"销量最佳的程序。罗维奥公司表示,到今年年底,安卓网站上的免费版本带来的广告收入每个月也有100万美元。

罗维奥北美业务开发部负责人彼得·维斯特巴卡表示,这个游戏的起源就是一位罗维奥设计师勾勒出的有着愤怒表情的红色小鸟。"当时我们大脑里还没有这个游戏的概念,但大家喜欢鸟,整个游戏情节也围绕鸟展开。"

维斯特巴卡称,公司当时注意到皮克斯动画电影的复杂情节,还有马里奥兄弟角色的流行程度。而《愤怒的小鸟》中的小鸟们除了表示愤怒的聒噪和咕哝就没有其他的了,不过玩家们似乎对此产生了共鸣。维斯特巴卡表示:"当成千上万的人穿的和游戏中的角色一样,你就知道在做的事情是正确的。"

目前罗维奥游戏公司正试图利用现有的成功将游戏移植到台式机和游戏机上,并生产小鸟、小猪的毛绒玩具,还希望为此拍摄电影或儿童电视剧。

卡耐基梅隆大学教授杰西·谢尔专门研究游戏设计和娱乐技术。他表示:"罗维奥让小鸟愤怒起来是个出色的创意。你可以把它们乱扔,没关系。试想,如果游戏主角是可爱的小鸟,在某种程度上可以说有趣,但大多数人多少都会有点排斥。"

More to Read

《愤怒的小鸟》的成功使得我们认识到,传统的销售模式——将游戏放入盒中,标价50英镑出售——已经过时了。《愤怒的小鸟》于2009年12月进驻苹果"App Store"应用商店,开始了艰难的起步。之后又进军"Android"市场,登陆跨平台应用商店"GetJar"。凭借这种创新的业务模式,《愤怒的小鸟》取得了巨大成功。而罗维奥游戏公司也开始憧憬建立一个像迪士尼那样的娱乐帝国。今年《愤怒的小鸟》将登陆全球最大的社交网站"Facebook",之后还将进军游戏机、电影、电视剧等领域。更为重要的是该公司与用户建立了积极的、持续的联系,不断发布最新消息。公司团队努力回答玩家通过"Twitter"和电子邮件提出的每一个问题,他们将粉丝设计的关卡添加到游戏中,并就小鸟的创意与他们进行讨论。玩家们感觉到,这是一家值得关注的游戏公司。

透视 PERCEPTION

Reading Guidance

关于凯特王妃与威廉王子的浪漫情事，人们早已津津乐道。然而，凯特是怎样从一个灰姑娘变成了时尚偶像和现代王妃，个中秘密却一直是令粉丝们猜不透的谜。自从凯特·米德尔顿挽着那被称为"世界上最具价值单身汉"——威廉王子的手臂踏上世界的舞台，整个世界的目光再没有离开过她。凯特之所以被世人喜爱是因为她是独立的职业女性——但更重要的原因是她并非生于贵族家庭。她的故事是现实世界中的童话。当凯特开始在圣安德鲁斯大学攻读学位的时候，她可能想明不到自己的生活所发生的改变会超越一切认知。与皇位第二顺位继承人陷入爱河之后，她也从未料想到8年之后的自己会成为皇室王妃，更不曾想过有一天自己能成为一个时尚偶像，而且作为世界各地妇女的榜样被世人所敬仰。

London Designers Hail "Elegant" Kate Middleton

Inspiring, chic and effortlessly elegant—that's what designers at London Fashion Week have hailed Kate Middleton's style, as her sartorial choices could prove a potential stimulus to Britain's clothing industry.

Middleton has graced magazine covers since she announced her engage-

ment to Britain's Prince William and her wedding in April was watched by millions of people around the world, with many eagerly waiting to see her bridal gown.

With all eyes on her wardrobe, dresses have sold out hours after she has worn them as women seek to copy her style. "I think she is the new queen of fashion… She's young, she's every little girl's dream and she always looks chic and sophisticated," Britain's Julien Macdonald said after his spring/summer 2012 womenswear show.

Middleton is as likely to wear designer clothes as high street ones. The 29-year old, now known as the Duchess of Cambridge, has been praised for wearing more affordable main street labels and has been snapped wearing clothes by British fashion retailers Reiss as well as Whistles and Spain's Zara.

A blue Issa knee-length dress that she wore when her engagement to William was announced sold out within 24 hours and cheap knock-offs vanished almost instantly. "I think she is great, I'm very fortunate that she likes to wear Issa," the label's designer Daniella Helayel told Reuters.

London has overtaken New York as the world's fashion capital for 2011, fueled by media interest in late British designer Alexander McQueen and Middleton, according to a survey by the Global Language Monitor released in August.

But while London has produced some of fashion's biggest names, it has struggled to maintain a global profile on a par with the other fashion capitals. Gloom on the high street is also evident. Consumer purchasing power is being squeezed by higher prices, muted wage growth, a lack of credit, job insecurity, a stagnant housing market and government austerity measures.

Could Middleton be the stimulus to Britain's fashion industry? "She has already been a stimulus," British Fashion Council Chairman Harold Tillman said. "What it has done, it's (given) the opportunity to teach the world again what Great Britain is about. It's not just about her, they're a good looking couple, they set each other off very well."

While no one denies Middleton's influence, fashion experts still debate her status. In New York, fashionistas said she was a style follower, not a trendsetter like her spouse's late mother Princess Diana.

But London-based designers were full of praise for her.

"I think she's brilliant, she's brilliant for England. Perfect, perfect future Queen, she's elegant, she knows how to hold herself," said Alice Temperley, whose white dress Middleton wore to watch the tennis at Wimbledon earlier this year. That dress also swiftly sold out online after Middleton wore it.

Middleton's wedding dress, by Sarah Burton for Alexander McQueen, has become one of the most talked about outfits of the decade and her style has been welcomed as an antidote to excess.

"There's nothing trashy or vulgar about her," Anna Wintour, the editor of *Vogue*, has been quoted as saying. "She dresses her age and never looks out of place."

Notes

sartorial:服装的
stagnant:停滞不前的
austerity:(经济的)紧缩

英伦设计师盛赞优雅凯特

时髦、自然、优雅，让人心动，这是伦敦时装周的设计师们对凯特·米德尔顿着装风格的称赞，她的着装选择将可能成为英国服装产业的潜在推动力。

自从米德尔顿和英国威廉王子宣布订婚之后，她就开始频频在杂志封面上亮相，她2011年4月份举行的婚礼吸引了全世界数百万人的目光，许多人都期待一睹她的新娘礼服。

凯特的衣着打扮已经成为众人瞩目的焦点，每款衣服一经她穿过就在几小时内全部卖光，女人们都争相模仿她的穿着。英国设计师朱利安·麦克唐纳德在他的2012春夏女装展结束后说："我认为她是新一代的时尚女王……她年轻，是所有小女孩的梦想，而且她看起来永远是那么时尚雅致。"

米德尔顿会穿设计师专门设计的服装，也会穿购物街上买来的衣服。这位29岁的剑桥公爵夫人因为身穿平价大众品牌的衣服而受到称赞，她曾被拍到身穿英国时装零售品牌"Reiss"和"Whistles"还有西班牙品牌"Zara"的服装。

与威廉公布订婚消息时，她穿了一件"Issa"品牌的蓝色及膝裙，据说24小时内就售罄，连廉价的仿制品也几乎被立刻抢购一空。该品牌的设计师丹尼拉·赫雷尔告诉记者："我认为她很棒，她喜欢穿'Issa'品牌的衣服是我的荣幸。"

全球语言监测机构8月份发布的一项调查结果显示，由于媒体对已故英国设计师亚历山大·麦昆和米德尔顿的关注，伦敦已赶超纽约成为2011

年的世界时尚之都。

但当伦敦诞生了一些时尚大牌的时候,这个城市不得不努力保持与其他时尚之都一致的国际地位。商业街上的阴郁气氛显而易见。消费者的购买力被多重挤压——高昂的售价,停滞不前的工资水平,信用额度缺乏,不稳定的工作,低迷的楼市,政府的经济紧缩政策。

米德尔顿能否成为英国时尚产业的强心剂?"她已经成为了一剂强心针,"英国时尚协会主席霍兰德·特尔曼说,"现在的情形已经使得世界再次了解英国。这不是她一个人的力量,他们夫妻二人俊男靓女,相映生辉。"

尽管没有人质疑米德尔顿的影响力,时尚专家们对她在时装领域的地位依然存在争议。纽约的时装评论家说她是一个潮流跟随者,而不像她丈夫的已故母亲戴安娜王妃那样是引领潮流的人。

然而伦敦的设计师们对凯特赞誉有加。设计师爱丽丝·坦波丽说:"我认为她很出色,对于英国而言很出色。是完美的未来王后,她很优雅,举止得体。"今年早些时候,米德尔顿曾身穿坦波丽设计的白色裙子去观看温布尔顿网球公开赛,之后这条裙子就迅速在网上销售一空。

米德尔顿的婚纱出自亚历山大·麦克奎恩公司的莎拉·波顿之手。这件婚纱已经成为近十年来最受瞩目的衣服,她的风格也被认为是对极繁主义的最好诠释而受到欢迎。

有人援引美国《Vogue》杂志的编辑安娜·温图尔的话说:"她丝毫不会给人廉价或低俗的感觉,她的着装和年龄相称,而且看起来永远是那么得体。"

More to Read

当21岁的凯特穿着透视装和黑色内衣为慈善活动轻快地走着猫步的时候,谁也想象不到有一天全世界的时尚编辑会关注她每一次的时尚动态。行业顶尖设计师叫嚣着学习她的穿衣风格,购物街充斥着"凯特式"的单品。凯特王妃荣登时尚杂志《名利场》公布的"2011年全球最佳衣着品味人士榜"。同时上榜的还有美国第一夫人米歇尔·奥巴马和法国第一夫人卡拉·布吕尼。在与第一夫人们同台竞艳的过程中,凯特王妃以超高"衣Q",引领起一股"平价"风潮。只要她穿过的衣服,立刻都会被抢购一空。众多人士认为,她的出现将会影响英国乃至全球的时装经济。凯特无疑正在树立一种属于自己的结合了坚定信仰和自然稳重气质的风格。她是世界各地的女孩的榜样。她自信、健康、独立,有一种经典的美,她是属于21世纪的王妃。

透视 PERCEPTION

Reading Guidance

美国电视分类中,情景喜剧(sitcom)、肥皂剧(soap opera)和情节剧(drama)三者都属于"电视连续剧"范畴。其中情景喜剧(situation comedy)作为一种喜剧演出形式,最初出现在广播中,后来逐渐成为最受欢迎的电视节目形式之一,在世界范围内被广泛接受。作为流行文化的一种表现,情景喜剧特别受到青年人的喜爱。象牙塔中的莘莘学子对流行文化的热衷是否意味着经典文学魅力的消退?大学生们严肃的学术研究是否会被淹没于喧嚣的电视文化?本文作者是一位文学课教授,把情景喜剧《老友记》引入了课堂讨论,以激发学生们对莎士比亚经典作品的热情。

A Classroom Tool for Opening up Shakespeare: The Sitcom

The future of literary studies is up for grabs. In his *The Rise and Fall of English*, Robert Scholes expressed the fear that English departments were about to go the way of classics departments, shrinking into insignificance, unless they learned how to change. The answer, I would argue, is hidden in plain sight: on TV and at the movies.

What our students love, and what we know how to teach, after all, are almost the same. And while this may outrage some literary purists, the future of English departments depends on our ability to link the two kinds of stories.

The popular television sitcom *Friends*, for example, is a contemporary variation on Shakespeare's melodramatic comedy *Much Ado About Nothing*. Never mind that the settings are different (Renaissance Italy, contemporary Manhattan), or that one is written in poetry and the other in the language of everyday life. The core characters, plots and themes are almost the same.

One reason for the parallels is that all comedies share certain qualities, especially those written on the pattern established by Roman New Comedy. Young lovers get together over the objections of their parents or their community, usually by clever trickery, and at the end there is a wedding or weddings, when everybody and everything is reconciled. Many sitcoms and movies are just as dependent as are the great dramatic comedies of the past, although in those meant for family audiences.

But *Friends* shares much more with Shakespeare than the tradition of New Comedy. It is *Much Ado* adapted to current economic and cultural conditions, and to the demands of the half-hour sitcom.

In *Friends*, as in *Much Ado*, a small group of unmarried young men and women flirt with each other, play a series of tricks on each other and fall in and out of love. Some characters are apprehensive and fearful about marriage and commitment, others more enthusiastic, but all are torn between the conflicting obligations of love and friendship.

Weddings end in disaster (Rachel's and Ross's, to name only—five). A man (Chandler) keeps women at a distance with his compulsive joking. Men and women (Ross and Rachel, Chandler and Monica) become romantically involved only when they learn by accident or unplanned confession how much each loves the other. A woman (Rachel) who has been badly hurt by the man she loves (Ross) requires that he suffer in abject humiliation before she will accept him again. A young couple are torn apart by jealous. A woman who is quiet and conventional slowly begins to gain confidence and, with it, her voice.

Ross loves Rachel in the first few seasons of the sitcom just as Claudio loves Hero in Shakespeare's comedy. The men are painfully shy, unsure of themselves because of their limited experience with love, and more than a little awkward. The women are young, beautiful, and gradually getting to understand and accept their qualities beyond that beauty.

In both cases, the characters are contrasted with their opposites. In Shakespeare, Claudio's comrades are the sexually active and witty Benedic, and Don Pedro, a man expert at wooing women and eager to help his friends. In Friends, Ross's pals are the sexually active, goofy Joey, who is usually successful with women, and the witty Chandler, who seldom is. Among *Much Ado*'s women, Hero is complemented by the outspoken, independent Beatrice. In *Friends*, Rachel has the outspoken, offbeat Phoebe and the independent Monica.

Four friends in Shakespeare become six on prime time, but the dynamics among them are similar. Chandler is the sitcom's version of Benedic—the witty, sarcastic bachelor who keeps himself from getting attached to women by obsessing over their faults. Benedic finally meets his match in the strong and clever Beatrice, who ultimately marries him, just as Chandler finally finds Monica. And through it all, Phoebe wanders like a typical Shakespearean fool, making off-the-wall comments and singing wacky songs that contain more than their share of truth.

In my classes, I grant equal time to *Much Ado* and *Friends*, even though it means I will have that much less time to devote to some other literary masterpiece. My students love *Friends*. The students are more apprehensive about Shakespeare, concerned as they are about the language they must master, the characters to keep straight and the exam looming on the horizon.

What they most want to talk about and understand is the television pro-

gram, while what I want to talk about and have them understand is Shakespeare. We meet in the middle.

I'm not tricking my students. *Friends* isn't simply an entree into Shakespeare. Shakespeare is also an entree into *Friends*. Shakespeare is the best way for them to fully appreciate something that enchants them and is an important part of their lives.

After dissecting both works, I ask my students the toughest question I know: Who gets the better story, the Elizabethan who attended a production at the Globe 400 years ago or someone who watches the American sitcom on a regular basis? Are we being cheated today?

My students are divided on the issue: Some are clearly disappointed in *Friends*, say they can watch TV no more and feel distressed at the loss of language in the past 400 years. Others are enchanted by *Friends* and say they have recruited others to watch it as well, so impressed are they by the ways in which Shakespeare can be adapted to the demands of contemporary American television. But in either case, I've won a victory: I have shown them that literary criticism is not simply a skill that allows them to get good grades in English courses, and that the great tradition of literature is alive and well, and worth knowing.

Because the entertainments that Americans love, and the great books that their professors know how to teach, are often similar in this fashion, popular culture can be the salvation rather than the nemesis of traditional humanities disciplines, particularly English.

Notes

reconcile:调和

compulsive:强迫性的,难控制的

dynamic:动态,相互作用的方式

apprehensive：忧虑的
dissect：详细评论，解剖

了解莎翁的新方式——情景喜剧

文学研究的未来掌握在大家手中。罗伯特·斯霍尔在《英语的兴衰》一书中表达了隐忧：英语系可能会步其他传统科系的后尘，变得越来越无足重轻，除非他们知道如何改变。我认为答案就藏在日常生活中——电视与电影。

学生们喜爱的，与我们擅长教授的，实际上并无二致。虽然这样说可能激怒一些文学清教徒，但英语系的未来就在于我们将这两者联系起来的能力。

比如深受欢迎的电视情景喜剧《老友记》就是莎士比亚情节剧《无事生非》的现代版。且不管故事场景不同（一个是文艺复兴时期的意大利，一个是当代曼哈顿），或是一个使用诗歌体，另一个全是日常用语。二者的主要人物、情节和主题如出一辙。

二者如此相似的原因之一在于所有的喜剧都具有共性，特别是那些按照罗马新喜剧的样式创作的作品。年轻的情侣不顾父母、家族的反对，想尽各种花招希望长相厮守。当所有冲突都解决的时候，故事就会以一个婚礼或是多个婚礼结束。许多电影和情景喜剧虽然面向家庭观众，但仍与古代的舞台喜剧一样以此为基础。

但《老友记》似乎偏离了新喜剧的传统而与莎士比亚的作品有着更多的相似点。它就是《无事生非》的剧本适应了现代经济文化条件，迎合半小时时长的情节喜剧的要求改编而成。

与《无事生非》相同，《老友记》讲述的是一群年轻男女互相调情，互相开玩笑,相爱又分手的故事。其中有人对婚姻与承诺充满担心、恐惧,有人则狂热积极。但他们都在爱情与友谊的责任和冲突中左右徘徊。

婚礼以灾难收场(仅瑞秋和罗斯两人名义上就有五次婚礼)。一个男人(钱德)强迫性地用玩笑与异性保持距离。男人、女人(罗斯和瑞秋,钱德和莫妮卡)在非常偶然的情况下,没有任何准备地告白,而开始恋爱。一个被自己的爱人深深伤害的女人(瑞秋),一定要在她的爱人(罗斯)经受了可怜的羞辱之后才肯再次接受他。年轻的夫妻因为嫉妒而分手。一个安静传统的女孩慢慢地建立自信,并表达自己的意见……

这部情景喜剧的最初几季中,罗斯一直爱着瑞秋,正如莎翁笔下的克劳迪一直爱着希罗。两个男人都非常害羞,因为没有足够的恋爱经历而缺乏自信,举止行为相当令人尴尬。两个女人年轻漂亮,慢慢地开始了解并接受美貌之外的魅力。

两个故事中,主人公都被辅以性格相对的角色。莎士比亚剧中,克劳迪的同伴是风流又智慧的培尼狄克,和乐于助人的求爱专家唐·佩德罗。在《老友记》里,罗斯的哥们一个是傻傻的乔伊,他风流倜傥,在女人方面频频得手,另一个是钱德,聪明却没有女人缘。《无事生非》里的女主角希罗与快人快语、性格独立的贝特丽丝形成互补。《老友记》中的瑞秋则与外向又另类的菲比和能干独立的莫妮卡形成互补。

莎翁笔下的四个朋友在当代的黄金时段变成了六人,但他们之间的互动与影响是相似的。钱德是情景剧版的培尼狄克——妙语连珠,喜欢挖苦人的单身汉,他总是专注于女性的缺点而无法爱上任何人。最终培尼狄克遇到了强势聪明的贝特丽丝,两人喜结连理——就像钱德后来找到了莫妮卡。整部剧中,菲比的角色就像莎士比亚剧中典型的傻瓜,做出稀奇古怪的评论,唱出怪异的歌曲,却蕴含着深刻的道理。

课上,我分配给《无事生非》和《老友记》相同的时间,即使这意味着我没有太多时间讲解其他文学名著。学生们喜爱《老友记》。莎士比亚则令他们忧虑,学生们担心要掌握的剧中台词,要了解的人物特征,还有早晚要面对的考试。

他们最想讨论的是电视节目,而我想让他们讨论和理解的是莎士比亚。我们各退一步。

我并没有欺骗学生们。《老友记》不仅仅被用来讲解莎士比亚的《无事生非》,《无事生非》也被用来讲解《老友记》。读莎翁的作品是他们充分理解他们所喜爱的情景喜剧的最好方式,也是他们生活的重要部分。

分析两个作品之后,我会问一个自认为最难的问题:谁看到了更好的作品,是400年前在伊丽莎白时代的环球剧场看戏的古人,还是按时收看美国情景喜剧的现代人?我们今天被欺骗了吗?

学生们对此持有不同观点:有的对《老友记》十分失望,表示不想再看电视了,对过去400年间丢失了美妙的语言感到遗憾。有的人被《老友记》深深吸引,还请更多的人一起观看,他们惊叹于把莎士比亚戏剧改写为当代美国电视节目的巧妙方式。在任何一种情况之下,我都是赢家——我向学生们展示这样一个道理,文学批评不仅仅是让他们在英语课上获得高分的工具,伟大的文学传统仍然有极强的生命力,值得学习。

由于美国人所喜爱的娱乐节目和大学教授所熟知的经典作品通常具有相似性,因此流行文化能够成为传统人文学科尤其是英语文学课堂的救世主,而非令人叹息的灾难。

More to Read

《老友记》是深受美国乃至全世界观众喜爱的情景喜剧,播出10年,共236集。剧中6位年轻人的感情起伏、事业波折和生活中的喜怒哀乐,加上轻松幽默的人物对白,故事中蕴含的"美式幽默",吸引了大批观众。10年间,剧中人物与观众们共同成长,如同美国社会文化的一面镜子。这部电视剧也被法国权威电影杂志《电影手册》评价为情景喜剧的里程碑。然而,这篇文章给了我们一个全新的角度来认识《老友记》——这个充满当代美国流行文化元素的剧集竟与莎翁名剧《无事生非》有着惊人的相似。作者将二者的人物与人物关系进行对比,清晰地展示出文学经典的魅力与生命力,以及文学批评的广泛性。看似枯燥高深的理论与经典,其实与生活现实息息相关,帮助我们获得独特深刻的思考。

Reading Guidance

英文中"奢侈"(luxury)本是一个拉丁词,原意指"极强的繁殖力",后演变为浪费、无节制,确切地说,这个词被用来描述在各种商品的生产和使用过程中超出必要程度的费用支出。这种支出是否值得,为什么会有那么多人愿意消费这样的产品?奢侈品牌的巨幅广告解释着时尚的含义,激励着人们的欲望。如今,奢侈品的消费群体变得更为宽泛和年轻,其中不乏省吃俭用的工薪族。一些深谙名牌之道的人超越了以物论物的阶段,声称会透过名牌看经济背景、人性善恶,看生活方式的不同表现,看名牌所蕴藉的文化内涵……但,还是有人会禁不住问:这些品牌凭什么那么贵?

Lo'and Behold

The other day, I saw a Louis Vuitton handbag with a price tag of $750 locked inside a department store glass case, and, I confess, I coveted the thing. The bag was made of laminated canvas, was covered with muddy LV monograms, and resembled, in shape and size, a beach tote—none of which attributes are especially prepossessing. And yet, I wanted it. Why? Why, for that matter, are so many women willing to spend a small fortune on bags emblazoned with Gucci G's, Chanel reverse-facing C's, and Hermes perforated H's?

The rise of the logo as a source of appeal took off 30 years ago in response, I would postulate, to a new kind of consumer that came into being with the investment-driven economy of the 1980s. Before that, old-moneyed people were content to know that their things were better made (and more expensive) than those of the hoi polloi, while new-moneyed people were content to engage in conspicuous consumption, flaunting their cars and their jewels in the time-honored fashion of the nouveau riche.

But in the 1980s, a new kind of new-moneyed class emerged with a more savvy relationship to consumerism. Maybe because they all had MBAs, they wanted to advertise their wealth in a more efficient and succinct way. Hence, the birth of the logo.

The trend began quietly enough, making its first appearance in menswear. The first stirrings can be traced to the custom-made shirt with its monogrammed breast pocket—though the monogram here was of the buyer, not the seller. But it was the Lacoste crocodile that was the real harbinger. The little croc on the breast pocket of a men's tennis shirt marked its wearer as "preppy"—a sportive type with a trust fund, as *The Official Preppy Handbook*, published in 1980, informed us.

As the success of *The Official Preppy Handbook* indicated, a *new* new-moneyed class had arisen that, though they didn't have trust funds, wanted to be preppies. In other words, they didn't want to engage in simple conspicuous consumption as their nouveau riche forerunners had done. They instead wanted to appropriate the style associated with old money. The solution, as they came to understand it, lay in surrounding themselves with the right sorts of things.

Traditional European fashion houses like Louis Vuitton, Chanel, Prada, and Hermes, and eventually, even the stodgier British and American companies like Burberry and Coach, understood this and began to market their products in

new ways: They did this by making their goods more instantly recognizable—aggressively promoting their distinctive aspects: the ridiculous horsey designs on the Hermes scarf; the dangling leather tags on the lead-heavy Coach bag; the dowdy plaid of the Burberry raincoat—all became emblems of old money exclusivity, marketed through trendy campaigns and ingenious product placement to the new masters and mistresses of the Universe.

The high-end companies that didn't understand went under. Logos are the quickest possible means of making clear that a product has the right provenance—i.e., comes from an exclusive place. And one of the salient characteristics of the new logo-ed merchandise is that it encourages "graded" purchase. Training goods prepare the less well-endowed for what is hopefully to come. Thus, those aspiring to wealth can buy the Louis Vuitton key chain, wallet, and, in a splurge, the handbag, while those who have definitively "arrived" can buy the full set of Louis Vuitton luggage—also, the Chanel suit and the Hermes Kelly bag with its distinctive lunchbox shape.

But capitalism is also resourceful in underhanded ways, and no sooner did the logo make an appearance on luxury goods than imitation logo-ed goods began to flood the market. I recall that in the 1990s one could buy a very nice imitation Gucci bag for $30 from a street vendor on the corner of 53rd and Fifth in Manhattan. Since then, in a predictable counter-move, the manufacturers of high-end merchandise have gone to court to stop the imitators, which means that you now have to make a real effort to find the knock-offs, and, when you do, you have to pay more for them. That $30 imitation Gucci that I could have bought on 53rd and Fifth 15 years ago would now cost at least $100 and take some looking for on the Lower East Side.

You probably couldn't find a better expression of capitalistic enterprise in action than the various moves and countermoves involving logo-ed merchandise, where value is continually undergoing revision and re-appropriation. And it's amazing that I can write this and still covet a Louis Vuitton handbag. Karl Marx would say that I've succumbed to the delusional effects of the bourgeois marketplace, the LV bag being just about the purest example there is of "exchange value"—an item entirely severed from its use value. I know I would do as well hauling my junk around in a plastic bag, but that doesn't prevent me from wanting a Louis Vuitton handbag.

Notes

covet：贪求，觊觎
monogram：字母组合图案，花押字
flaunt：夸耀
nouveau riche：暴发户的
stodgy：无趣的，无生气的
dowdy：穿着单调过时的
re-appropriation：重新拨款使用

看那些名牌！

有一天，我看见百货商场的一个玻璃柜里锁着一只路易·威登手包，包上挂着750美金的价签，我承认自己十分觊觎这个东西。这款包是压层帆布的，印着暗灰色的"LV"花押字，形状和大小都很像一个沙滩包——没有一样让人特别心动。但是，我想买。为什么呢？为什么那么多女性都甘愿花费不菲的价格去买那些标有古琦"双G"，香奈尔正反相对的"双C"，爱马仕打孔"H"图案的手袋？

我猜想，以商标作为装饰的热潮始于 30 年前，是与 20 世纪 80 年代投资驱动型经济下形成的一种新型消费者紧密相关。在此之前，旧富满足于自己的东西质量比普通民众的更好（价格也更贵），而新贵们则更喜欢夸耀型消费，以那种历史悠久的暴发户方式炫耀他们的名车和珠宝。

但在 20 世纪 80 年代，新一代新贵阶层出现了，他们具有更精明的消费理念。或许因为他们都是工商管理学硕士，也都希望以更有效、更简明的方式展示自己的财富。因此，商标装饰应运而生。

这一趋势开始得悄无声息，首先出现在男装上。最初的迹象可以追溯到顾客定制衬衫胸袋上的纹章装饰——当时的花押字是顾客姓名的首字母而不是商家的"logo"。法国鳄鱼品牌是真正的先行者。在男式网球衫的胸袋上的小鳄鱼，标志着它的穿着者是有品味的新贵——热爱户外运动又多金，正如出版于 1980 年的《权威预科生手册》中描述的那样。

《权威预科生手册》这本书的成功标明新一代新贵阶层出现了，虽然他们没有太多财富，但仍希望成为品味一族。换句话说，他们不需要"暴发户前辈"们那种夸耀型消费，相反，他们要的是旧富那样的一种适合自己的风格。解决方案正如他们理解的那样，就是将自己置身于代表着积极身份的东西中。

传统的欧洲奢侈品牌，比如路易·威登、香奈尔、普拉达和爱马仕，以及更古板一些的英国和美国品牌巴宝莉和寇兹都认识到这一点，开始用新的方式营销自己的产品。他们把自己的产品变得更易于识别，积极地宣传自己的特点：爱马仕围巾上印着可笑的马匹图案；死沉死沉的寇兹包上挂着皮质吊牌；巴宝莉风衣印着老掉牙的格子纹——这些都曾是旧富的专属，通过时尚的营销方式和新的产品定位已经被新一代的世界主人们接受。

没有意识到这一点的高端公司纷纷倒闭了。商标以最简便的方式说明一个产品的来源——出身名门。这些带着商标的产品的一个重要特点是：它们鼓励了"分级"消费。入门级的产品是为那些不太有钱但将来可能会有足够消费能力的潜在顾客准备的，那些刚刚有点儿钱的人可以买路易·威登的钥匙链、钱包，或许挥霍一下买一只手袋；而那些确实已经"到达"这一消费层次的人能买一整套的路易·威登行李箱、香奈尔套装和爱马仕著名的午餐盒形状的凯利包。

然而资本主义在欺诈方面也表现得足智多谋。一出现带着商标的奢侈品,那些冒牌仿制品就开始充斥市场。我还记得20世纪90年代的时候,可以在曼哈顿53大街和第五大街的交口处,花30美金从街头小贩那里买到一个相当不错的假古琦包。但那之后,意料之中的抵制行动开始了,高端产品的生产商们走上法庭禁止所有的冒牌货。这就意味着,现在要想买到假名牌可得费一番工夫,15年前我可以在曼哈顿53大街和第五大街的交口,花30美金买到的假古琦,现在至少要价100美金,还得去下东区好好找找才买得到。

形形色色的商标博弈——除此之外,你可能找不到更好的表达来描述与对抗资本主义企业的行为了。在此博弈中,商标的价值被不断地修改和再分配。我一边写着这篇文章,一边觊觎一只路易·威登手袋,真是奇怪的感觉。卡尔·马克思也许会说我已经陷入了资产阶级市场制造的错觉之中,路易·威登包就是"交换价值"(一种与商品使用价值完全割裂的价值概念)存在的证明。我也知道直接把那些乱七八糟的东西装进塑料袋背着去这儿去那儿没什么不好,但这也不妨碍我想要得到一个路易·威登手袋。

More to Read

奢侈品牌制造者的主要工作不仅是设计、制造精良优美的产品,对市场的理解,对销售策略的把握往往比产品本身更重要。要让大多数人产生可望而不可及的感觉是奢侈品牌营销的使命。在市场定位上,要维护目标顾客的优越感,帮助他们建立身份认同,就要使大众与他们产生距离感。奢侈品牌似乎在不断地设置消费壁垒,拒大众消费者于千里之外。要使认识品牌的人与实际拥有品牌的人在数量上形成巨大反差,这正是奢侈品消费给我们造成的幻象。当手提路易·威登,身着香奈尔的人们穿梭于繁华街市时,那些时隐时现的"logo"似乎在宣布着主人的身份和品味。

Reading Guidance

  本文的主人公是阿历克斯·弗格森，一个面色赤红，嘴里永远嚼着口香糖的老头，他是世界上最成功的足球俱乐部的教练，他的球队被球迷称为曼联，也被称为红魔。摄影师们喜欢捕捉比赛时紧张地咬着自己的指甲的弗格森，和曼联进球后挥舞着拳头露出孩子般笑容的弗格森，而这个长着酒糟鼻的老头脾气异常火爆，他被称为更衣室里的"吹风机"，在那里他会愤怒地把球靴踢向大卫·贝克汉姆的额头。他喜欢看一部名为《塔加特》的侦探剧集，塔加特也成了弗格森的一个外号，而弗格森监视自己球员在足球场外一举一动的高超手段恐怕会让剧中的塔加特也望尘莫及。曼联巨星吉格斯年轻的时候每次周末出去玩，周一弗格森都能说出他去了哪里，和谁在一起。弗格森在球队的绝对权威容不得一点侵犯。这位一向不服输的苏格兰人还会和英超对手温格与穆里尼奥大打嘴仗。不过这一切基于他如此享受着足球带给自己的快乐。即使2011年10月23日在主场老特拉福德1:6惨败给同城小兄弟曼城，创下81年来主场失球的纪录，弗爵爷也没有因屈辱而倒下，用他的话说，我们还会获得英超冠军！

Man United!

  Ferguson celebrates 25 years in charge at Manchester United in November—the average tenure for a coach of one of England's premier clubs is just two years—and all reports of retirement continue to be greatly exaggerated. Having taken on all comers for a quarter of a century, and most often prevailed, Ferguson seems to have set his unbreakable will against aging and mortality. You wouldn't necessarily bet against him. He has already defied the laws of physics by creating what's known as Fergie Time, a phrase now common in England that describes the elastic interval that ensues after a match or event is supposed to have ended, but which, in fact, continues. Ferguson created "Fergie Time" out of sheer force of will. His mere presence on the sideline, staring obsessively at his watch, has often caused officials to create nonexistent seconds and minutes to allow Manchester United further time in which to prevail.

 In those minutes, magic often happens. The pattern was set in 1999. Ferguson's team, competing in the European champions' League final, the most coveted of all club titles, was losing by a single goal to the German side, Bayern Munich, and the match had all but ended. In desperation, Ferguson introduced two substitute players, as a last hopeless gamble. Within a properly miraculous minute, both players had scored, the adamantine German team had crumbled, and Manchester United had been crowned champions of Europe.

 The mythology of the club, a mythology that's been constantly renewed in Ferguson's years, lies in its special ability to exact triumph from disaster. This spirit took root in what happened to the Busby Babes of the 1950s: perhaps the greatest generation of young football players ever assembled at one club, by the manager Matt Busby. The team, mostly in their late teens and early 20s, and led by Duncan Edwards, arguably England's greatest young player, was already a legendary force when tragedy immortalized them. Taking off from an airfield in Munich in 1958, the plane on which they were traveling crashed, and eight of the young players, including Edwards, were killed. Busby, who was on life support for several days, survived, along with the talismanic player Bobby

Charlton, still a director at the club. Out of that wreckage, Busby eventually rebuilt a mesmerizing team around Charlton, which went on to triumph in the European Cup a decade later.

Subsequent managers were left to live up to that legend. Until Ferguson came along 20 years later, all had found different, dismal ways to fail. Fergie was handpicked for the role of second coming by Sir Bobby Charlton, now knighted, and the octogenarian Sir Matt Busby, then still at the club in an ambassadorial role. In the years since 1968, the club's fortunes had not only declined but, worse, those of its greatest rival, Liverpool FC, had risen. Ferguson—a working-class Scot, like Busby—came from Glasgow's Govan docks, the toughest quarter of what is consistently among the most violent cities in Europe. He arrived with one overriding ambition, which was to knock Liverpool off its pedestal. At the time the idea seemed laughable. United's rivals had won 16 national titles and five European titles compared with their own seven league titles and single European Cup win in 1968. This summer, however, Ferguson finally made good on his ambition, securing United's 19th domestic title, surpassing their intercity rivals by one. They remain two trophies behind Liverpool in Europe, and it is widely believed that Ferguson will not rest until that record is also put right.

It is the manner in which this formidable feat has been achieved, however, that makes Ferguson such a unique figure. In fact, his capacity for megalomania and anger invites comparisons with Shakespeare's more ferocious protagonists— Coriolanus, say. United players on the receiving end of their manager's ranting call it "the hair dryer" effect: up-close invective, most often administered at halftime, so moist and salty that it can ruffle even the most structured footballers' coiffures. His clashes with players over the years have inspired dark sagas that have run for weeks, sometimes months, on the back pages of the newspapers, the most memorable being his standoff with David Beckham, the poster boy of international soccer. After one match in which he felt Beckham,

透视 PERCEPTION

then the team's captain, had not earned his millions, Ferguson kicked at a stray boot in the locker room and the flying footwear hit Beckham over the eye, drawing blood. The pair had to be separated as they squared off.

Beckham, whom Ferguson had nurtured since the age of 11, but whose celebrity marriage to Posh Spice had somehow betrayed that trust, was brusquely sold to United's Spanish rivals, Real Madrid. It says a lot for the player—and perhaps for Ferguson—that Beckham repeatedly expresses his sustained admiration for his "father figure". That fierce loyalty is almost universal in Ferguson's teams.

If he has an almost unparalleled ability to renew and refresh teams—no manager in British football history has achieved his sustained success over more than a generation—he has also retained a core of players in whom he places his utmost faith and, whisper it, indulgence. For a while, Beckham was one of those chosen players. Some others include Roy Keane, a hard-drinking, hard-tackling Irishman of fearsome intensity who was perhaps the closest to him temperamentally; Ryan Giggs, a supreme athlete (of whom Ferguson said when he first saw him as a 13-year-old that "he floated across the ground like a cocker spaniel chasing a piece of silver paper in the wind"); and Cristiano Ronaldo, a virtuoso Portuguese runner, full of toreador trickery on the ball, who has been key to the renaissance of the last decade, before Ferguson sold him reluctantly, again to Madrid, for a record-breaking £80 million. On the current team, the much-tattooed Wayne Rooney, a working-class hero whose spirit is matched by his skill, is the talisman.

Over the years, there have been many outrageous feuds: with the BBC, to which Ferguson has refused to speak since 2004, over a perceived slight of his son in a documentary; with match officials (on a weekly basis); and with rival managers, particularly Arsène Wenger of the London club Arsenal, who is yin to Ferguson's yang—deeply cultured, professorial and similarly insane to win. This maddening intractability has been more than compensated, however, with

continuing moments of grace and occasional genius, and above all a life-affirming refusal to go gently. Time eventually gets called on even the greatest of sporting careers, but Fergie Time seems to go on forever.

Notes

tenure：任期
adamantine：坚定的
mesmerize：使着迷
octogenarian：八旬老人
overriding：首要的
megalomania：自大狂

男人，曼联！

到11月份，弗格森就已经在曼联俱乐部待了整整25年了——英超俱乐部教练的平均任期只有两年，关于他退休的传闻也是愈演愈烈。与后辈晚生较量了四分之一个世纪之久，且胜多败少，弗格森似乎以自己坚不可摧的意志对抗了衰老和命运。和他打赌，你很难赢。他甚至创造出所谓的"弗格森时间"来否定物理定律，这个已经在时下英格兰成为常用短语的表述方式是指伤停补时在本该已经结束时却依然延续。弗格森全凭顽强的毅力创造了"弗格森时间"。当比赛时，他只是站在边线处，着魔一般看着自己的手表，在这种强大气场的压迫下，裁判通常会不自主地多补上分秒时间，而曼联则会利用多出的丁点时间完成绝杀。

短暂的几分钟时间里，经常会有奇迹发生。这种模式始于1999年。当时弗格森的队伍一路杀入欧冠决赛，有望一举捧得所有俱乐部最梦寐以求的冠军头衔，但在决赛中，他们却以一球落后于德国的拜仁慕尼黑队。眼看着比赛即将结束，在绝望中，弗格森孤注一掷派上两名替补球员。在神奇的最后一分钟内，曼联依靠这两名替补连入两球，彻底摧垮了素以意志顽强著称的德国球队，成功加冕为欧洲冠军。

弗格森执教的这些年中，曼联在不断创造各种神话，但这家俱乐部最大的神话莫过于它从灾难走向成功的能力。这股精神来源于20世纪50年代"巴斯比的孩子们"的不幸遭遇。当时的教练马特·巴斯比将一批有史以来最为优秀的青年球员集中于曼联，他们大多20岁上下，但在队长邓肯·爱德华兹——这位英格兰最伟大的年轻球员的率领下，已经被认为是一支传奇队伍，然而悲剧最终降临在他们身上。1958年，曼联队员们所搭乘的飞机在慕尼黑机场起飞时冲出跑道撞毁了，包括爱德华兹在内的8位年轻球员遇难。主教练巴斯比经过数日抢救之后幸存了下来，当时一同幸免于难的还包括伟大的球员博比·查尔顿——他至今仍在担任曼联俱乐部董事。空难以后，不屈不挠的巴斯比围绕着查尔顿又组建了一支全新的曼联，并在10年之后勇夺欧洲俱乐部杯赛冠军。

人们期待继任的教练能够延续巴斯比的传奇。然而直到弗格森接手俱乐部时的20年间，这些教练都以不同的方式凄凉地失败了。当时，已晋升为爵士的博比·查尔顿钦点了弗格森，而已入暮年的马特·巴斯比爵士还在担任俱乐部大使的角色。自1968年夺冠以后，俱乐部一直在走下坡路，而且更糟糕的是，他们的头号死敌利物浦队开始崛起。和巴斯比一样出身于工人阶层的苏格兰人弗格森，来自于格拉斯哥的高文港区，此地一直在欧洲最暴力城区之列。弗格森初来之际就立下一个压倒一切的目标——把利物浦队从王座上拉下来。在当时，这种想法看似荒唐可笑——利物浦队已经赢得了16次联赛冠军和5次欧洲冠军，相比之下，曼联只拿到过7次联赛冠军和1968年的一次欧洲冠军。不过，今年夏天，弗格森终于实践了自己当初立下的豪言壮语——曼联拿到第19个联赛冠军，比死敌利物浦队多拿了一次。但在欧洲赛场上，他们仍比利物浦队少拿两次冠军，人们普遍认为，在追平这项纪录以前，弗格森是不会退休的。

弗格森获得丰功伟绩的独特方式让他成为了一个特立独行的人物。事实上，甚至有人将性格狂妄暴怒的弗格森与莎士比亚笔下的残忍角色科利奥兰纳斯相提并论。在更衣室中领教过主教练咆哮的曼联球员们甚至用"吹风机"一词来形容他近距离的恶语谩骂。弗格森通常是在半场休息时发威，其猛烈程度连某些球员最纹丝不动的发型也会被吹乱。多年以来，弗格森与球员们之间发生的冲突衍生出很多阴暗的传说，这些话题经常会连续几个星期，甚至是几个月地刊载在报纸的末版上。其中，最令人难忘的就是他与足球界的偶像人物大卫·贝克汉姆之间的对峙。在一场比赛之后，弗格森认为担任队长的贝克汉姆不够卖力，便在更衣室中踢飞了一只球鞋，刚巧击中了小贝的眉头，小贝顿时血流满面。之后，两人关系剑拔弩张，最终分道扬镳。

贝克汉姆从11岁就开始在弗格森手下踢球，但他与辣妹维多利亚的结合却在一定程度上辜负了这份信赖。随后，贝克汉姆转会曼联在国际赛场上的主要对手——西班牙的皇家马德里。但他却时常把对弗格森这位"父亲般人物"的钦佩之情挂在嘴边，这种强烈的忠诚感在弗格森的队伍中十分普遍。

弗格森不仅在球队重建和球员更新上拥有近乎无可匹敌的能力（在英国足球史上，没有哪位主教练能像他那样在几代球员身上持续取得成功），他在挽留核心球员方面同样出手不凡。在这些球员身上，弗格森倾注了极大的信任，也可以说是放纵。曾几何时，贝克汉姆也是这些被器重的球员中的一位。此外，还包括罗伊·基恩，这位嗜酒如命、球风硬朗的爱尔兰球员，脾气火爆，性格和弗格森最为接近；瑞恩·吉格斯，一位超级球星（弗格森曾说过，他第一次见到13岁的吉格斯时，发现"他飞奔在草地上，就像在风中追逐锡纸片的小猎犬"）；克里斯蒂亚诺·罗纳尔多，拥有大师般球技的葡萄牙球员，他是过去10年来曼联复兴的关键人物，之后弗格森以破纪录的8000万英镑的价格，不情愿地将他卖到了皇家马德里。还有当前曼联队中满身文身的韦恩·鲁尼，这个来自工人家庭的球员球技一流且意志坚定。

透视 PERCEPTION

多年以来，围绕着弗格森发生了很多让人瞠目结舌的纷争：自 2004 年以来，弗格森一直拒绝接受英国广播公司（BBC）的采访，原因是他觉得英国广播公司的一部纪录片对其子进行了污蔑；他与比赛裁判之间的冲突（几乎每周上演一次）；他与对手教练之间的矛盾，尤其是阿森纳的主教练温格，他们二人的风格一阴一阳——温格气质儒雅，学者风范，二人的共同之处在于温格也执著地渴求胜利。弗格森令人抓狂的倔强脾气与他带来的无数辉煌时刻、难得一见的天赋以及拒绝妥协的人生态度相比可谓微不足道。即便是最伟大的体育生涯也终有落幕的一天，但"弗格森时间"似乎会一直延续下去，直到永远。

More to Read

　　这篇文章的题目"Man United"很明显变化自曼联队的英文名称"Manchester United"，以此为题可谓简洁、风趣又能突出文章的中心。短短千字，弗格森的巨大成就与乖张不羁的性格跃然纸上，他教练生涯中的重要时刻也被一一提及，可谓重点突出又趣味盎然。值得一提的是，1999 年 12 月，弗格森被白金汉宫授予爵士爵位，从而成为正式册封的英格兰足球功勋人物，载入史册。在足球历史上，主教练获得这样的荣誉，弗格森独一无二。毫不为过地说，弗格森不仅是曼联俱乐部历史上最伟大的教练，英国足球历史上最成功的教练，也是世界足球最伟大的教练之一，登峰造极的一代宗师。

Reading Guidance

在什么地方能看到世界上的思想领袖、商业精英、艺术奇才、文学大家等各路好手汇聚一堂？非"TED 大会"莫属。从 1990 年开始，"TED 大会"每年在加州长滩举办一次，比尔·克林顿、比尔·盖茨、维珍品牌创始人理查德·布兰森、国际设计大师菲利普·斯达克等都曾经担任过大会的演讲嘉宾，大会也被参加者们称为"超级大脑 SPA"和"未来四日游"。"TED"是英文"technology"、"entertainment"、"design"三个单词的首字母缩写。"TED 大会"是社会各界精英交流的盛会，它鼓励各种创新思想的展示、碰撞。不过"TED"再精彩，也不过是一个封闭的精英俱乐部，大家关起门来享受思想的乐趣。从 2006 年开始，"TED"陆续将多年录制的新旧演讲视频传到网上，供人免费观看和下载。本文介绍了"TED"组织的一次广告竞赛，从中可以看出"TED"所关注的层面越来越广，涉及的领域也由以前的学术、艺术拓展到更多元的文化认知。

A Contest to Find Ads Worth Passing on

The nonprofit organization TED, whose tagline is "ideas worth spreading", has decided to spread something else: advertising.

At the annual TED conference in Long Beach, Calif., organizers are to announce the winners of the inaugural TED Ads Worth Spreading Challenge, a contest the group began in December to get advertisers to create online marketing videos that people actually want to watch, said Chris Anderson, the curator of the conference.

"Let's not make it the same conversation we're having on TV," Mr. Anderson said. "It's not an ad, it's an idea. It's not an ad, it's a story."

The ubiquitous presence of video on the Web means that advertisers need to think of new ways to engage their audiences. The idea of the contest was for ad creators to go beyond the 30-second spots that viewers usually associate with television commercials or the 15-second spots that run before a video online.

"Part of this is really about starting a conversation about advertising," said Ronda Carnegie, the head of global partnerships for TED, a conference originally known as Technology, Entertainment and Design. "Advertising is just not about selling you something. It really has to give you something back in order to reward the attention you give it."

On the TED Web site, which features online video seminars, ads are shown after a video is watched, not before. The longer form ads can also help "humanize a company," Mr. Anderson said. "In the long term, it's good for TED to be a place where people can expect the ads they see are as compelling as the content."

The ad challenge was open to anyone and was free to enter. Among the 1,000 submissions collected from December through February, 10 winners and 14 honorable mentions were selected by a panel of 24 judges that included advertising and media executives, video artists, filmmakers, journalists and producers.

According to TED representatives, 40 percent of the submissions came from major brands, 30 percent from small businesses, 40 percent were from nonprofits or were public service announcements, and 10 percent came from students and advertising schools. The video submissions varied in length from

30 seconds to five minutes.

TED also teamed up with YouTube on the project. "The fact that they are seeing ads as a critical part of the cultural landscape, that seemed like a natural fit for us," said Eric Meyerson, group manager for video advertiser marketing at YouTube. "A lot of publishers really recognize that the world comes through YouTube-defined video."

The TED channel is one of the most popular channels on YouTube, Mr. Meyerson said. On March 18, YouTube will showcase the winning videos in a special section on the YouTube home page. On March 22, YouTube will host an event for the winners at the Art Directors Club in New York City.

Judges were asked to look for submissions that were powerful and memorable enough that a typical TED audience member would feel compelled enough to pass it on.

"We're very much interested in pushing advertising forward," said Paul Kemp-Robertson, the editorial director of *Contagious* magazine in London and a contest judge. In judging the ads, Mr. Kemp-Robertson said he asked himself questions like, "Would I want to look at it again? Would I want to share it? Would I see it as redefining advertising as an industry?"

One of Mr. Kemp-Robertson's favorite ads was a spot that generated a lot of attention during the Super Bowl because of its length of just over two minutes. The ad for Chrysler called *Born of Fire*, by the agency Wieden + Kennedy, featured the rap star Eminem driving a Chrysler through the streets of Detroit on a gray winter day.

"That had a resonance way beyond the Super Bowl," Mr. Kemp-Robertson said, "It was like 'OK, we're back.' This is the sprit of America, the muscle."

Mr. Anderson said the ad fulfilled the goal of rebranding an entire city and not just an automobile company. "It felt gritty, it felt honest, it felt really powerful," he said.

Another ad featured Dulux, a line of decorative paint from Akzo Nobel. The spot was a stop-motion video of people from Brazil to India using brightly colored paint to cover up blighted areas.

In addition to the YouTube promotions, the winning submissions will receive multiple prizes, including their own Web page on TED.com for one year and will be used as ads on TED.com from March 21 to 27.

Notes

curator:(博物馆、美术馆)馆长
ubiquitous:无所不在的
blight:使枯萎

竞赛——寻找值得传播的广告

以"传播值得传播的思想"为口号的非营利性机构"TED",决定传播一些其他的东西——广告。

一年一度的"TED大会"将在加州长滩举行。该组织的负责人克里斯·安德森说,届时,大会组织者将宣布在"TED值得传播的广告"大赛中的获胜者。该竞赛从去年(2010年)12月开始,要求参赛者制作出人们真正想看的网络营销视频。

"不要把它做成电视上的那种陈词滥调,"安德森先生说,"这不是广告,而是思想。这不是广告,而是故事。"

广告在互联网上无处不在,这意味着广告商需要出新求变来吸引观众。这一竞赛的主旨就是让制作者们创作出能够超越那些观众经常在电视上看到的 30 秒商业广告或者在网上视频开播前的 15 秒广告的优秀作品。

"TED"全球合作伙伴领导人隆达·卡内基说："在很大程度上，这次竞赛是要开展一个与广告的对话。广告不仅仅是向你推销某种产品。广告应该能够回馈你对其投入的关注。""TED"大会的名字来源于英文"技术"（technology）、"娱乐"（entertainment）和"设计"（design）三个单词的首字母。

以播放在线讲座为特色的"TED"网站上，广告出现在每段视频的最后，而不是开始。这些加长版的广告也能"使一个公司变得更人性化"，安德森先生说："从长远角度看，如果'TED'能够成为一个广告与内容同样精彩、令人期待的地方那就太棒了。"

这次大赛向所有人免费开放。从去年 12 月至今年 2 月共收到 1000 件参赛作品，由包括广告媒体管理者、影像艺术家、电影导演、记者和制片人在内的 24 人组成评审团，从参赛作品中评出 10 个优胜奖和 14 个优秀奖。

据"TED"公司代表说，40% 的参赛作品来自著名公司，30% 来自小型企业，40% 来自非营利性组织或是公益组织，还有 10% 来自学生和广告学院。参赛视频时长 30 秒到 5 分钟不等。

"TED"和"YouTube"合作了这个项目。"实际上，他们把广告看作文化背景的一个重要部分，这与我们的想法不谋而合。""YouTube"视频广告部市场经理埃里克·梅尔森说："许多出版商都意识到整个世界都在看'YouTobe'式的视频。"

梅尔森先生说，"TED"频道是"YouTobe"上最热门的频道之一。3 月 18 日，"YouTobe"将在主页开辟一个专门版面，展示大赛获胜视频。3 月 22 日，还将在纽约艺术导演俱乐部为获胜者举办一场活动。

评委们需要在参赛作品中遴选出最有力、最令人难忘的视频，这些视频能让一个典型的"TED"观众觉得非常愿意与他人分享。

"我们对推动广告业的发展非常感兴趣，"伦敦《行销杂志》编辑主任、本次大赛的评委之一保罗·肯普—罗伯逊说。在评判参赛作品的时候，肯

透视 PERCEPTION

普—罗伯逊先生说他会先问自己一些问题，比如："我会再看这个广告吗？我会把它推荐给别人吗？我会觉得它能够重新定义广告行业吗？"

肯普—罗伯逊最喜欢的作品之一是在"超级碗"冠军赛中插播的一则广告。该广告引起了人们极大的关注，因为它只有两分钟。它由韦登迪广告公司为克莱斯勒公司制作，名为"浴火重生"。广告由说唱明星艾米纳姆担纲，他在一个灰蒙蒙的冬天，开着一辆克莱斯勒汽车穿过底特律的大街。

"它比'超级碗'比赛还能令人产生共鸣，"肯普—罗伯逊说，"这就像在说'好吧，我们回来。'这是美国的精神，强悍有力。"

安德森先生说这个广告取得的效果不仅重塑了一家汽车企业，还重塑了一个城市的形象。他说："它坚定、真实、有力。"

另一个是阿克苏诺贝尔公司旗下的多乐士的广告。这则单格拍制的广告展示了从巴西到印度，人们用亮丽的油漆粉刷衰落城区的景象。

除了"YouTube"的推荐以外，获奖作品还可获更多奖励，包括在"TED"网站上对其网站为期一年的宣传，以及3月21日至27日期间，直接作为广告出现在"TED"网站上。

More to Read

创立于1984年的"TED"，原本是一个技术性的聚会。2002年，克里斯·安德森几经周折从古怪的老设计师理查德·威曼手中买下"TED"之后，力排众议，把它改造成了一个开放和多元化的大会。邀请的演讲者从原先的技术、娱乐、设计三个领域扩展到了各行各业，科学家、哲学家、艺术家、探险家、心理学家、语言学家、宗教领袖、音乐家、慈善家……在安德森看来一切知识都不是孤立的。每一个问题，都可以往许多个不同的方向去寻找答案。如今，"TED"已成为一个跨界的智库，一个对话的平台。

Reading Guidance

"Lady Gaga"这个名字到底该怎样翻译？有人译为"女神嘎嘎"，认为她时尚前卫、歌舞了得，是个"女神"、"女王"；还有人译为"雷得嘎嘎"，称其衣着、行为怪异，实属"雷帝"、"雷母"。因嘎嘎造型惊人，台湾媒体还授其"搞怪女王"的称号，至于嘎嘎的粉丝则自称"小怪兽"，直接把偶像视为"怪兽之母"。然而，许多人对嘎嘎存在一定的误读。例如认为她出身穷困，以致衣着古怪随便；她音乐素质低，只能靠奇装异服吸引眼球。但实际上，女神嘎嘎出生于纽约富裕家庭，从小读的都是学费高昂的贵族学校。她天资过人，4岁学会弹钢琴，而且是无师自通，13岁开始作曲和演出，17岁被纽约大学音乐系提前录取，20岁便签约为黑眼豆豆、小甜甜布兰妮等红星写歌；全美大热的《绯闻女孩》和《一个购物狂的自白》等电视剧的主题曲也出自女神嘎嘎之手。有人预言女神嘎嘎将是麦当娜的接班人，也有人认为她不过是昙花一现。究竟该如何解读她？阅读本文可以帮助我们透过嘎嘎浮华百变的造型，了解这位才华横溢的歌手。

Get Your Ph. D. in Lady Gaga

Sometime in 2008, the world entered the age of Lady Gaga. She seemed to spring from the Billboard charts fully formed, microphone in hand at the ready.

Details of her pre-Gaga biography began filtering out: Her birth name is Stefani Germanotta, she grew up in New York and dropped out of NYU. Anyone with an Internet connection can see YouTube clips of the days before she commanded the attention of music critics and clubgoers alike, and her outfits turned into something from Coco Chanel's nightmares. But the essence of Gaga remains mysterious: She is an enigma wrapped inside a glass-shard-studded suit, singing maddeningly catchy dance tunes about monsters. Perhaps it's this disconnection between the Gaga of 2010 and the videos of conventionally pretty Germanotta sweetly playing piano that has led to so many theories about her.

Why is Lady Gaga worth studying?

Pop matters. We needed a pop star who could simultaneously celebrate the spirit of pop—the spirit that makes everyone, no matter who or where they are in the world, stand up and start dancing when *Billie Jean* comes on the jukebox—and deconstruct, and ultimately shift, the static notion of the pop star as a figure of blind worship. Gaga has put the glitter wand back into the hands of the audience. She's made the audience responsible for what they are viewing. No other pop singers are doing that, at least not on the level that Gaga is.

Some people accuse Gaga of being a poseur, not a performance artist.

When saying this, they miss the point of her project. Gaga's about faking fame, and she doesn't claim to be genuine. We definitely find her performance to be consciously a pose. That's part of her goal: to demonstrate how powerful the artificiality is.

Gaga has so often been compared to Madonna, and wrongly dismissed as a Madonna clone. Both Gaga and Madonna are transformative artists, but unlike Madonna, Gaga makes her entire life a performance. For example, Gaga's outfits physically distort the female figure to the extreme, and she often wears clothing that's physically dangerous. There's a combination of human and animal (such as her lobster hat, or her Hello Kitty gown), and of human and machine (such as her famous iPod glasses). Madonna always looked sexy no matter which period she was in. Gaga seems to be evolving toward something beyond sexy.

If we look at the careers of other artist such as Bob Dylan, Madonna or David Bowie—all famous for their constant transformations—we'll find that their careers each have a number of personal genres or phases; they'll spend some time writing a certain style of music and performing an accompanying persona, and then they'll move on to a new style after a while. But Lady Gaga's transformations are all at once: she's a multiplicity of genres and styles and ideologies at the same time.

Lady Gaga has inspired more academic readings of her work than other current pop stars. Part of it is the way that Gaga appropriates symbols and value systems for her act: Mickey Mouse, Star Wars, freemasonry, capitalism, consumerism, Quentin Tarantino, Stanley Kubrick, Michael Jackson, Madonna, Christianity, monarchy, to name a few. Taken piecemeal, they totally contradict each other. But together, they create a cohesive picture of Gaga. She embodies a number of oppositions: sacred and profane, man and woman, sexy and horrifying. Her performances continually underscore her ambivalent nature; she can't be defined.

She also demonstrates the way fame functions; how we're obsessed with spectacle. Lady Gaga enjoys the benefits of being a pop star while simultaneously revealing those trappings to be poisonous, frivolous, murderous and fake. It's something that many conceptual artists do: they deconstruct ideology by too loudly chanting ideology's slogans, or too blatantly displaying its symbols. Gaga dressed up as a queen when she performed for Queen Elizabeth, and fashioned herself as Barbara Walters when she was interviewed by Ms. Walters herself.

Gaga said to an interviewer at CNN: "I am whoever you perceive me to be." She reflects back the things society projects onto pop stars. By drawing attention to her self-conscious performance of fame, she gives power to her audience. Lady Gaga doesn't announce the death of the pop star; she demonstrates the strength of the spectacle in our culture.

Notes

enigma：谜
static：静止的
poseur：装腔作势的人
appropriate：挪用，盗用
frivolous：轻率的

重新认识女神嘎嘎

2008年的某个时刻，世界进入了女神嘎嘎时代。她似乎手握麦克风直接从公告牌排行榜上走下来。她成为女神嘎嘎之前的历史逐渐清晰起来：她本名斯蒂芬妮·杰尔马诺塔，生长在纽约，从纽约大学退学。任何人如果可以上网都能在"YouTube"上看到她的视频，那还是她开始吸引乐评人和夜店客之前的表演，而后她的着装逐渐变成了可可·香奈尔的噩梦。但是嘎嘎的本质仍然令人难以捉摸——她是一个裹在用碎玻璃片装饰的外套里的谜，唱着关于怪物的舞曲，这些歌曲令人疯狂又朗朗上口。2010年的嘎嘎和视频上那个温柔地弹着钢琴的传统美女杰尔马诺塔截然不同，或许正是这种断裂感使得人们对她有各种猜测。

为什么女神嘎嘎值得研究？

流行音乐很重要。大家需要一个流行明星来自然随心地倡导流行精神——这种精神会使得每个人，不论是谁，不论在世界的哪个地方，一听到点唱机里响起《比利·珍》就会站起来，开始跳舞——同时，这个人还能解构并最终改变流行明星作为盲目崇拜对象的固有偏见。嘎嘎把闪闪发光的魔杖交还听众手中。她使得观众对自己所看的内容负起责任。没有其他流行歌手做到这一点，至少没有人达到嘎嘎的层次。

有人指摘嘎嘎哗众取宠，不是真正的表演艺人。

这样说的人并不理解嘎嘎的做法。嘎嘎要表现的正是虚假的名声，她也从未标榜自己真实。我们确实会发现她的表演就是有意识地作秀。这是她的目的之一——展示人工制造的力量。

嘎嘎经常被拿来和麦当娜相比，也常被误解为麦当娜的克隆。虽然她们两个都是划时代的艺人，但与麦当娜不同的是，嘎嘎将自己的整个生活都当做表演。比如嘎嘎的造型将女性的身体形态扭曲至极致，她常穿的衣服可能会对身体造成伤害。她的造型有的把人类与动物结合（比如她的龙虾帽子、凯迪猫造型的长裙），有的把人类与机器结合（比如她著名的"iPod"造型的眼镜）。麦当娜在任何时候都打扮得很性感，而嘎嘎似乎已经超越了性感。

如果我们看看其他艺人的艺术生涯，比如鲍勃·迪伦、麦当娜或是大卫·鲍伊——他们都以风格百变著称——我们会发现在他们的艺术生涯中都有很多创作期和创作风格；他们会在一定时期内创作某种风格的音乐，展现出相应的个性，一段时间后会过渡到新的风格。但是女神嘎嘎所有的变化都是同时发生的——她是不同风格、不同流派和不同意识形态的结合体。

女神嘎嘎比同时代的其他流行明星引发了更多的学术关注。原因之一在于嘎嘎把象征符号和价值体系融合到了她的行动中：米老鼠、星球大战、共济会制、资本主义、消费主义、昆汀·塔伦蒂诺、斯坦利·库布里克、迈克尔·杰克逊、麦当娜、基督教、君主制等。单独看来它们格格不入，但掺杂在一起，就形成了嘎嘎一贯的风格。她体现出很多的对立面：圣洁与下流，男人与女人，性感与惊悚。她的种种表演不断地强调其矛盾的本质——她无法被定义。

她同样展示了名誉是如何被利用的；我们对哗众取宠的热闹场面是如

何着迷。女神嘎嘎很享受作为流行明星的种种益处,同时她也在揭露那些圈套的毒害性、草率性、凶残性和虚假性。这是很多概念艺术家所做的事情:他们通过大声重复某种意识形态的口号或简单铺排它的各种标志来解构这一意识形态。嘎嘎打扮成女王的样子为伊丽莎白女王表演,打扮成芭芭拉·沃特斯接受沃特斯女士的采访。

嘎嘎在接受国际新闻网(CNN)记者采访时说:"你认为我是谁我就是谁。"嘎嘎将社会投射在流行明星身上的形象反射回去。她将人们的注意力吸引到自己身上,故意表演出名的种种状态,她赋予观众力量。女神嘎嘎并没有宣告流行明星的死亡,她表现了我们文化中哗众取宠具有的力量。

More to Read

女神嘎嘎的横空出世既是美国摇滚精神的延续,更有商业化操作的考量。已成符号的女神嘎嘎之于流行文化而言,更像是一场精心操控的行为艺术,她和她的言行是对一个高度信息化、虚拟化、数字化时代的强烈反讽,她必须不断变换造型才跟得上人们瞬息万变的喜好,才能在信息爆炸的当下引发人们对自身卑微存在的确认和共鸣。无论如何,这都是一个让人惊叹的时代,出名、出位已经不仅仅需要野心和勇气了,它还需要货真价实的才华和足以说服自己并抵挡各种非议和谩骂的强大承受力。嘎嘎在接受媒体采访时说:"我每天扯各种谎……我,女神嘎嘎也是个谎言,只要你真心相信自己会成功,这谎言终是会成真的。"

Reading Guidance

当苏珊大妈走上舞台，一鸣惊人，实现自己的梦想又令全世界感动的时候；当《幸存者》成为年度最受欢迎的节目时；当《非诚勿扰》的男女嘉宾成为人们茶余饭后的谈资时，我们知道电视真人秀的时代到来了。美国著名人类学家米德早在20世纪70年代就曾预言，这种新的电视形式必将流行。真人秀强调实时现场直播，没有剧本，不是角色扮演，是一种声称百分之百反映真实的电视节目，迎合了普通人猎奇、八卦、偷窥他人隐私的心理。观众厌倦了虚假的电视剧，厌倦了造作的演员，厌倦了千篇一律而巧合得天衣无缝的剧情，观众需要一种接近真实，百分之百原汁原味，没有演员、没有编导、没有剧情的节目，这就是真人秀。

The Reality Principle

On January 6, 1973, the anthropologist Margaret Mead published a startling little essay in *TV Guide*. Her contribution, which wasn't mentioned on the cover, appeared in the back of the magazine. Mead's subject was a new Public Broadcasting System series called *An American Family*, about the Louds, a middle-class California household. "Bill and Pat Loud and their five children are neither actors nor public figures," Mead wrote; rather, they were "the members of a real family". Producers compressed seven months of tedium and turmoil (including the corrosion of Bill and Pat's marriage) into twelve one-hour episodes, which constituted, in Mead's view, "a new kind of art form"—an innovation "as significant as the invention of drama or the novel".

An American Family was a hit, and Lance Loud, the oldest son, became a celebrity, perhaps the world's first openly gay TV star. But for decades *An American Family* looked like an anomaly; by 1983, when HBO broadcast a follow-up documentary on the Louds, Mead's "new kind of art form" seemed more like an artifact of an older America. Worthy heirs to the Louds arrived in 1992, with the début of the MTV series *The Real World*, which updated the formula by adding a dash of artifice: each season, a handful of young adults were thrown together in a house, and viewers got to know them as they got to know one another. It wasn't until 2000, though, that Mead's grand claim started to look prescient. That year, a pair of high-profile summer series nudged the format into American prime time: *Big Brother*, a Dutch import, was built around surveillance-style footage of competitors locked in a house; *Survivor*, a Swedish import, isolated its stars by shipping them somewhere warm and distant, where they participated in faux tribal competitions. Both of these were essentially game shows, but they doubled as earthy anthropological experiments, and they convinced viewers and executives alike that television could provide action without actors.

We are now more than a decade into the era that Mead saw coming. "I think we need a new name for it," she wrote, and in the past decade we have mainly settled on "reality television", although not without trepidation. "Reality" is, if not quite a misnomer, a provocation—a reminder of the various constraints and compromises that define the form. Certainly, "reality television" is an amorphous category; Mark Andrejevic, a cultural theorist, notes that "there isn't any one definition that would both capture all the existing genres and ex-

clude other forms of programming such as the nightly news or daytime game shows." If Mead were alive today, she might be surprised at the diversity of the form, which has proved equally hospitable to glamorous competitions, like *American Idol*, and to homely documentaries, like *Pawn Stars*, which depicts the staff and clientele of a Las Vegas pawnshop.

One of the biggest differences between today's reality television and its 1973 antecedent is the genre's status. Having outgrown PBS, it has inherited the rotten reputation that once attached to the medium itself. In an era of televised precocity—ambitious HBO dramas, cunningly self-aware sitcoms—reality shows still provide a fat target for anyone seeking symptoms or causes of American idiocy; the popularity of unscripted programming has had the unexpected effect of ennobling its scripted counterpart. The same people who brag about having seen every episode of *Friday Night Lights* will brag, too, that they have never laid eyes on *The Real Housewives of Atlanta*. Reality television is the television of television.

No surprise, then, that a counter-movement has arisen, in the form of books that urge us to take these shows more seriously. Jennifer Pozner is a journalist and activist, and in the past decade she has watched, by her count, "more than a thousand hours of unscripted programming," which is a lot if you think of it as work, but not much—two hours per week, which may be less than the average American watches—if you don't. For Pozner, it certainly was work. The book she wrote about her experiment is *Reality Bites Back: The Troubling Truth About Guilty Pleasure TV*, and, halfway through, she sums up her verdict: "I've found most of it painful, aggravating, or mind-numbingly boring."

Notes

turmoil：混乱，骚动

pawn：典当

antecedent：前事，前情
aggravate：使恶化，激怒

真实原则

1973年1月6日，人类学家玛格丽特·米德在《电视导报》上发表了一篇令人震惊的短文。这篇文章在杂志封面上并未被提及，它出现在那期杂志的后面。文章所讨论的对象是一部由美国公共广播公司新推出的电视系列剧《一个美国家庭》，电视剧讲述的是一个加利福尼亚的中产阶级家庭——劳德一家的故事。米德写道："比尔·劳德与帕特·劳德和他们的五个孩子既不是演员也不是公众人物。"确切地说，他们是"一个真实家庭的成员"。制作人将历时7个月拍摄到的冗长而混乱的素材（包括比尔和帕特的婚姻危机）剪辑成12集节目，每集时长一个小时。米德认为，这是"一种新的艺术形式"——这一创新的"重大意义可与戏剧或小说的出现同日而语"。

《一个美国家庭》风行一时，大儿子兰斯·劳德成为了名人，他可能是世界上第一个公开自己是同性恋的电视明星。但几十年来，《一个美国家庭》都是一个另类。1983年，"HBO"播放了劳德一家的纪录片续集，米德眼中的"一种新的艺术形式"更像是一件来自昔日美国的手工艺品。真正继承劳德一家衣钵的是1992年于"MTV"电视台首播的系列剧《真实的世界》。这部系列剧和《一个美国家庭》相比在形式上有所变化，增加了一些人为控制因素：每一季，一群年轻人聚集在一个房间里，观众们慢慢了解他们正如他们了解彼此。直到2000年，米德伟大断言的预见性才开始显现。那一年，两部备受瞩目的夏季系列剧将此种形式推向了美国的黄金时段：

《老大哥》，荷兰出品，以监控录像的形式展开，所有竞争者被封闭在一个房间里；《幸存者》，瑞典出品，选手与世隔绝，被送到一个温暖而遥远的地方，参与人为设计好的类似于部落竞争的比赛中。这些节目本质上都是游戏竞技，但是增加了人性实验的因素，也使得观众和电视台主管们确信电视可以没有演员。

如今我们进入米德所预言的时代已经十多年了。她曾说："我们需要为它命名。"过去十年来，固然不太确定，但我们还是称之为"真人秀"（reality television）。"真实"（reality）这个词虽然不是非常不妥，但却提示了界定这一形式时面临的多重限制和妥协。当然，"真人秀"类别中包括的样态并无定式；文化理论家马克·安得耶维奇说道："并没有一种定义能够囊括现存所有类型，同时排除其他类型，诸如晚间新闻和日间游戏等。"如果米德还健在，她一定会为真人秀形式的多样性所惊奇。既有《美国偶像》这样奢华靓丽的竞赛；也有《典当之星》这样朴素平实的纪录片，讲述拉斯维加斯一家当铺的员工和客户的故事。

现在的真人秀与其1973年的"前辈"相比，最大区别在于这一节目类型的地位。真人秀节目已经摆脱了美国公共广播公司的模式，却承袭了曾一度依加在电视这一媒体上的坏名声。在一个以电视展示制作才能的时代——比如雄心勃勃的"HBO"电视剧，设计巧妙具有强烈自我意识的情景喜剧——真人秀成了被人指摘的靶心，被认为是美国人愚蠢的表现或是造成美国人愚蠢的原因。令人始料未及的是，没有剧本的节目大受欢迎的同时，也使得那些有剧本的节目显得高尚起来。吹嘘自己从不错过任何一集《胜利之光》的人，也会向人夸耀他们从来不屑于真人秀节目《亚特兰大娇妻》。真人秀是电视中的电视。

不出所料，一股对抗性的运动已经兴起，有人以书的形式号召大家要严肃地看待真人秀节目。詹妮弗·波兹内是个记者和活动家，根据她的说法，过去十年间她看了"超过一千个小时没有剧本的节目"，如果把看这些节目当做工作，数量确实惊人；但如果不是工作的话，每星期两个小时就不算太多，远远少于美国人看电视的平均时间。对波兹内来说，这是项工作。她出版了有关她的实验的书《现实的回击：罪与乐的电视的困惑真相》。行

透视 PERCEPTION

文至中,她总结了她的意见:"我发现大部分节目给人带来痛苦、愤怒,抑或是无聊到让人大脑麻木。"

More to Read

真人秀以戏剧化的真实性、刺激的窥视性和激烈的竞争性,吸引了全球亿万观众的眼球,成为电视界赚取高额利润的一个热门节目形式。然而对它的批评也不绝于耳。真人秀带给观众的满足感既可能与社会的文化内涵、价值理念相协调,也有可能与其南辕北辙。这使得美国的真人秀节目自诞生之日起就争论不断。很多人认为节目赚取的哭声、笑声或是叹息声都是廉价的,缺少文化底蕴的支撑,所以注定不会长久。甚至有些节目趣味庸俗,被指挑战道德底线,不得不草草收场。相反,一些制作精良、内涵深厚的传统电视节目,历久弥新,受到大众喜爱。或许,一个丰富多彩、包罗万象的电视业态,能够为观众提供各种选择,满足不同层次、不同年龄观众的需求,才是大家所希望看到的。

Reading Guidance

"脸谱"是什么？它是将近7亿用户的资料整合在一起，不仅了解他们住在哪儿，朋友是谁，还知道他们对什么感兴趣，在线上做什么的网站。在它创办至今（2011年）的7年里，其注册用户如果以人口数量算，它是地球上的第三大国；如果以人口分布广度计算，即使是16世纪的西班牙和19世纪的大英帝国也无法与之比肩。"脸谱"是全球最大的社交网站，也许是人类历史上由完全不同的人聚合在一起的速度最快的团体，也是今天互联网上最大的分享网站。马克扎克伯格是谁？生于1984年的他是目前全球最年轻的亿万富翁，根据资本市场的估算，如今他的身家已达120亿美元，而为他攫取巨大财富的便是社交网站"脸谱"。他少年得志，以至于保罗·艾伦评价说："我无法在世界历史上找到一个先例，这么年轻的人却拥有这么大的影响力——等一等，只有一个人，那就是亚历山大大帝。"不过，历来媒体对于2004年2月4日在哈佛宿舍推出"脸谱"网站以前的马克·扎克伯格报道甚少，本文将视线聚焦在马克·扎克伯格的高中时代，借此更多地了解"脸谱"和他的创始人。

Did Mark Zuckerberg's Inspiration for Facebook Come Before Harvard?

The stories we hear these days about Zuckerberg in popular media tend to follow a common sensationalist pattern: super-smart kid invents a tech phenomenon from his Harvard dorm room, drops out, and changes the world. It's a classically framed, Bill Gates-esque story of success driven by intelligence and ambition. What's most intriguing about the Zuckerberg story, however, isn't that he dropped out of Harvard and became a billionaire at 23.

The reason we hear so little about Zuckerberg's pre-launch vision for Facebook is likely because he has been a controversial target over the true origins of his business. In 2007, several of Zuckerberg's classmates came forward and claimed rights to the Facebook idea after reports surfaced that Yahoo had offered $900 million to purchase Facebook just two years after the founding of the company. Even though the suit against Zuckerberg was settled last year, given the nature of the proceedings, we'll likely never get an official answer from Zuckerberg himself about the true origins of his inspiration. But maybe we don't need one after all?

It turns out that Zuckerberg's academic history offers a great deal of insight into the inspiration for Facebook and why it was so wildly successful when it first launched. February 4th, 2004 may mark a major milestone in Facebook's history, but the story of Mark Zuckerberg's rise to fame in fact starts years before he stepped foot on the Harvard campus, and is much more complex and interesting than is usually portrayed.

Pre-Zuckerberg: Tracing the roots of Facebook culture

You may be surprised to hear that while Harvard was fertile ground for the launch of Facebook, the seed of the concept was likely planted in Zuckerberg in high school. You never hear about Zuckerberg's alma mater Phillips Exeter Academy in stories because Harvard was where the action really started. But in fact, the time that Zuckerberg spent at the academy from 2000 to 2002 likely had more influence on the name and initial concept of Facebook than any of his classmates at Harvard.

Phillips Exeter Academy (or "Exeter") is a private boarding school for grades 9 to 12, located in Exeter, New Hampshire. The prestigious prep school is a member of the Ten Schools Admission Organization. Like the other "Big Tens", Exeter has a tight-knit boarding community that lives on campus full time. Students refer to themselves as "Exonians".

An Exonian for two years, Zuckerberg had plenty of time to observe and participate in the social culture and rhythms ingrained in Exeter's boarding lifestyle. Every year, the school says goodbye to a few hundred students and welcomes a few hundred more. Zuckerberg enrolled in the fall of his junior year and, like every new and returning student, received his own copy of Exeter's student directory, "The Photo Address Book", which students affectionately referred to as (you guessed it) "The Facebook".

We interviewed several of Zuckerberg's peers this week, and they all confirmed what David Farrant (class of 2000) had to say: "The front cover says 'The Photo Address Book', but we all called it 'The Facebook' all the time because 'The Photo Address Book' was such a mouthful. Everybody called it that."

"Facebook" photo directories were (and still are) a huge part of the students' social experience and culture at prep schools such as Exeter. Every school in the Big Ten prints and distributes one for its students annually. Because students aren't allowed cell phones on campus and living accommodations are in such flux from year to year (they change houses and phone numbers annually), these "Facebooks" are a valuable resource for students.

Of course, not only do students need the directory to find and contact their peers, but the books become part of the culture of bonding between classmates and friends, as students use it to see where their peers live, who's hot and who's not, who lives with who, and who the new kids are. Sounds an awful lot like how people use Facebook online now, right? Of course, it also describes an early pre-Internet social culture, facilitated by photo directories.

透视 PERCEPTION

A more complete picture of the Facebook success story

Now that Facebook has graduated from its academic roots and been released to the world for free, its continued growth has many experts saying it will likely be the dominant social platform for the foreseeable future. At 200 million users (and counting), Facebook makes it hard to doubt that it will have considerable influence in the way we all connect and communicate in the future, both locally and across borders. While we may never know the true origins of Mark Zuckerberg's inspiration for Facebook, looking at the social culture of the prep school he attended and his experiences as a boarding student there offer us insight into where the explosion of global Facebook culture may have begun, why it was so successful when it launched at Harvard, and how luck and opportunity may have led one of the world's youngest visionaries to start coding in his college dorm room.

Notes

controversial:有争议的
flux:不断的变化
visionary:有远见的人

马克·扎克伯格的灵感源头

最近主流媒体对扎克伯格的报道都难免落入了俗套——一个超级聪明的孩子在他哈佛宿舍里发明了一项了不起的技术,随之辍学,然后改变世界。这是一个典型的由智慧和雄心驱动的比尔·盖茨式的传奇。然而有关扎克伯格的成功故事,最吸引人的还不是他从哈佛辍学,在23岁成为亿万富翁。

我们很少听说扎克伯格推出"脸谱"网站之前的事情,也许是因为对于这个网站的想法是否来自扎克伯格还存在争议。2007年,在"脸谱"成立仅两年后,雅虎提出以9亿美元的价格收购这个网站,这时扎克伯格的几个同学站出来声称对"脸谱"网站的创意拥有所有权。尽管这场官司已经在去年得到平息,然而鉴于诉讼的性质,我们很可能永远无法从扎克伯格口中得知他灵感的真正来源。或许我们根本不需要他的回答。

事实证明,扎克伯格的高中时代为"脸谱"网站的起源及其迅速获得巨大成功的原因提供了重要线索。2004年2月4日或许是"脸谱"网站历史上的一个里程碑式的时刻,但是扎克伯格的成功故事早在他踏进哈佛校园几年之前就开始了,并且比我们了解的更加复杂有趣。

扎克伯格前传:探寻"脸谱"文化起源

也许你会觉得惊讶,虽然哈佛是"脸谱"成长的沃土,但其核心理念却产生于扎克伯格的高中时代。或许你对扎克伯格的母校菲利普埃克塞特高级中学知之甚少,毕竟哈佛才是他事业的起点。但事实上,从2000年至2002年,扎克伯格在埃克塞特中学度过的这段日子,对他在网站创建和命名上的影响远大于他的哈佛同学对他的影响。

菲利浦埃克塞特中学是一所面向9至12年级学生的私立寄宿中学,位于美国新罕布什尔州的埃克塞特市。该校享有很高的声誉,是十大名校组织成员之一。和其他"十大名校"一样,埃克塞特中学有个严谨的寄宿社区,学生住在学校里,自称为"埃克塞特人"。

在校两年期间,作为埃克塞特人的一分子,扎克伯格有充足的时间去观察和参与源于埃克塞特中学寄宿生活的社交活动。每年,该校都要迎来送往数百名新生和毕业生。高二那年秋天,同其他新生和返校生一样,扎克伯格收到了一本埃克塞特中学同学录——"图片地址花名册",同学们都亲切地称之为(你一定猜到了)"脸谱"。

通过采访扎克伯格的同级生,他们都证实了大卫·法兰特(2002届学生)的说法:"封面写的是'图片地址花名册',但我们一直都把它叫做'脸谱','图片地址花名册'太拗口了。大家都那么叫。"

"脸谱"图片地址花名册曾是(现在也是)诸如埃克塞特中学之类的私立中学社交文化的重要组成部分。所有"十大名校"每年都会为学生印制、发放一本。由于学生在校不许用手机,并且学生入学一年后要搬宿舍,因此"脸谱"就成为对学生来说极具价值的资源。

当然,学生们不仅需要同学录查找联系其他同学,这些同学录也成为同学和好友之间的文化纽带,因为学生用它来确定好友住在哪里,谁辣,谁丑,谁和谁住一间宿舍,谁是新来的。和现在"脸谱"网站的用法差不多,对吧?当然,这同时描绘了一个前因特网时代通过照片花名册辅助的社交文化。

更加完整的"脸谱"成功故事

现在,"脸谱"已从象牙塔走出,并且免费向全球开放。众多业内人士认为,由于"脸谱"网站的持续发展,在可预见的未来,该网站有可能成为占统治地位的社交平台。"脸谱"的用户已达2亿名(仍在不断增加),我们不会怀疑它将极大地影响我们所有人联系和通信的方式,无论是在本地还是跨越国界。尽管我们可能永远不知道扎克伯格创办这个网站的灵感来自何方,但当我们对他曾就读的埃克塞特中学,以及他作为寄宿生的经历有所了解,我们就能发现"脸谱"文化的起源,我们也能清楚地了解,为什么"脸谱"在哈佛推出时能一炮走红,以及何种运气和机遇让这位世界最年轻的幻想家之一能在大学宿舍里开始编写"脸谱"代码。

More to Read

　　马克·扎克伯格究竟从何处获得创办"脸谱"的想法？本文作者追溯到扎克伯格的高中时代，希望从中获得答案。如果看看根据扎克伯格的故事创作的电影《社交网络》你会发现一处很关键的情节，是马克·扎克伯格从温克莱沃斯兄弟那里剽窃了"脸谱"的基本创意。扎克伯格虽然受雇于温克莱沃斯兄弟，却对开发进度一拖再拖，背地里开发自己的项目，最终导致了原始项目的流产和"脸谱"的异军突起。而事实上，早在"脸谱"诞生之前两年，在斯坦福大学校园内，已经有一个叫做"Club Nexus"的在线服务采用了同样的机制。"脸谱"的创意究竟从何而来？或许只能期待扎克伯格自己来揭晓答案。

透视 PERCEPTION

Reading Guidance

随着亚马逊网上书店的"Kindle"等电子阅读器在多国流行,电子书不再是喜爱新技术的"极客"族群专属的阅读媒介,而逐渐成为主流阅读选择之一。相对传统出版业已有500多年的历史,亚马逊公司成立不过十余年时间,但创始人、现任CEO 杰夫·贝索斯却通过增加一系列新技术和新服务,找到了将步入暮年的出版业变成充满朝气的互联网业务的出路。电子书阅读器普遍拥有网络接入功能,可以在线购书。亚马逊网站提供的电子书达到 48 万册,巴诺提供的电子书加上电子杂志、报刊超过 100 万种,这使读者可以从容选择,让购书变得更容易。

In a Battle of the E-Readers, Booksellers Spurn Superheroes

  The tablet wars have begun. Superheroes are the prize—or perhaps the victim.

  Amazon, seeking to make its coming Kindle Fire tablet as appealing as possible, negotiated a deal with DC Comics for the exclusive digital rights to a hundred popular graphic novels. Among the series: *Superman*, *Batman*, *Green Lantern*, the *Sandman* and *Watchmen*.

Barnes & Noble, with a tablet of its own to nurture, did not like this one bit. Two weeks ago it removed all the copies of the physical volumes from its 1,300 stores, saying it would not carry any book if it were denied the right to sell the digital version.

Books-a-Million, the third-largest bookseller with 231 stores, followed suit last week, making the same argument.

Booksellers of all sorts used to pride themselves on never removing any book from their shelves, but that tradition is fading as competitive struggles increase. Last year, in a sort of foretaste of the present conflict, Amazon temporarily removed the "buy" buttons for the publisher Macmillan as part of a struggle over e-book pricing.

This time, the stakes are once again high. The two chains are desperate to avoid becoming showrooms for Amazon's digital warehouse, which would quickly send them to the bookstore graveyard like their former colleague Borders. DC Comics must stay relevant in a world where many of its young male fans read everything on mobile devices—not the most congenial medium for comics. And Amazon must preserve and extend its dominance.

In online comics forums and other places where the issue is being debated, everyone is unhappy with someone. Amazon is being accused by some of throwing its considerable weight around to the detriment of readers and the larger culture. DC Comics is being criticized by others of placing greed over its fans. Barnes & Noble is alternatively being accused of throwing its own weight around and of cutting off its nose to spite its face. Even the comics' writers are getting some heat.

As Amazon seeks over the next few years to expand its tablet line, these collisions over content are likely to become routine. "It looks like content providers and online purveyors have a few more rounds to go before the Wild West is tamed," said Lorraine Shanley, a publishing consultant.

DC Comics, a division of Warner Brothers, says it is being misunderstood.

透视 PERCEPTION

But on its own Web site, it said the books would be available "exclusively to Amazon's newly announced Kindle Fire," with no qualification. Even the possibility that fans could have access to the books on their iPads through the Kindle app seemed disallowed.

DC now says the books will be available on other e-readers through the Kindle app. "Just because we're starting with Amazon, this is not the be-all and end-all of our digital strategy and distribution," said Jim Lee, co-publisher of DC Entertainment, the parent company of DC Comics. He added, however, "We are not at liberty to discuss exactly when" the comics would be available on other e-readers, citing the company's nondisclosure agreement with Amazon.

Amazon declined to comment about the deal.

Independent bookstores, which are rarely offered exclusives by publishers, argue that they are bad for consumers.

"A competitive retail market where products are available from lots of different places creates greater choice and a competitive pricing environment," said Oren Teicher, chief executive of the American Booksellers Association. "Choice is better than no choice."

Some readers certainly feel that way. Neil Gaiman, the author of the *Sandman* series, wrote on his blog that he got a "strange deluge of hate mail" after posting on Twitter about the dispute. A sample letter: "I was very excited when I heard that *Sandman* was coming out as an e-book, but was heartbroken when it was announced that I and my kids won't have it on our readers."

Mr. Gaiman, who said he knew nothing about the Amazon deal until it was announced, was critical of Barnes & Noble. "As the author of 12 percent of the books in question, I couldn't understand why Barnes & Noble's reaction to Amazon getting a digital exclusive was to effectively give Amazon and the independent stores a physical exclusive as well, and then to publicize that," he wrote in an e-mail.

"On the other hand," he added, "they've made their point, and other

publishers will think twice before giving exclusives."

One group is watching the tablet war with a certain detached amusement: comic book stores.

"This fight between Amazon and Barnes & Noble is like the tide or a storm or an earthquake," said Jack Rems, owner of the Escapist Comic Bookstore in Berkeley, Calif.. "Nothing I can do about it."

Well, there is one thing. Escapist is offering 20 percent off all the DC titles that the chains removed. Mr. Rems said he hoped the deal would bring some new business in the door.

Notes

congenial：适宜的
detriment：损害
purveyor：供应商

电子读者的争夺战，超级英勇的牺牲地

平板电脑的战争已经打响。超级英雄们从中得利——抑或是成为牺牲品。

为了使即将推出的"Kindle Fire"平板电脑拥有更大的吸引力，亚马逊公司与"DC"漫画公司达成一项协议，即后者向其提供一百部深受读者喜爱的漫画书的专属数字版权，这其中就包括：《超人》、《蝙蝠侠》、《绿灯侠》、《睡魔》以及《守卫者》。

巴诺连锁书店也计划培养自己的平板电脑,因而对这一协议相当不满。两周前,该公司将所有"DC"漫画公司出版的实体漫画书从其所属的1300家店铺下架,声明如果巴诺连锁书店不能从"DC"漫画公司获得出售其漫画书数字版本的权利,他们将拒绝出售任何"DC"漫画公司出版的纸质书。

布米——拥有231家店铺的美国第三大图书销售商——出于同样的理由,于上周效仿这一举措也将"DC"漫画公司的图书下架。

各种类型的书商都曾经以图书不下架为荣,但是这一传统在面临日益激烈的竞争环境时已变得不合时宜。去年,或许可看做是当前冲突的一次预演,亚马逊公司与麦克米伦出版社因电子书价格发生冲突,暂时性移除了该公司图书在网站上的"购买"按钮。

这一次,其中的风险冲突更是变本加厉。两家连锁书店使出浑身解数,竭力避免自己沦为亚马逊数字图书仓库的展示厅,因为这情况一旦成真,它们将被迅速推向图书销售的墓地,重演边界连锁书店的悲剧。"DC"漫画公司必须跟上世界的发展,现在的小年轻们都用移动设备进行阅读——虽然这对漫画而言并非最适宜的媒介。而亚马逊公司,必须维持并扩展自身的统治地位。

这一话题正在网络动漫论坛以及其他场所被人们热烈地探讨,而每个人似乎都有所不快。有人指责亚马逊蛮横自大,置读者与文化利益于不顾;也有人指责"DC"漫画公司贪得无厌,伤害了粉丝的感受;巴诺则要么被指为独断专行,要么被批评搬起石头砸了自己的脚。甚至动漫作者们也没能逃过这一劫。

亚马逊公司计划在接下来几年里不断扩大它的平板电脑生产线,此类冲突很有可能成为常态。"如今看来,在野性的西部被征服之前,内容提供商与网络平台商之间还要进行几轮角力,"出版顾问洛兰·尚利这样说。

作为华纳兄弟的子公司,"DC"漫画公司表示自己被误解了。然而在其网站上,公司声明读者只能在亚马逊新推出的"Kindle Fire"上无限制地阅读这些书籍,而使用"iPad"的动漫粉丝们,他们即使通过"Kindle"的应用程序也无法获得这些资源。

"DC"漫画公司解释说,这些书籍以后将可以通过"Kindle"应用软件在其他电子阅读器上呈现。"DC"漫画公司其母公司"DC"娱乐公司的共同发行人吉姆·李说:"只是因为亚马逊公司是我们最初的合作伙伴,目前的做法并非我们数字战略与发行销售的唯一途径。"不过他接下来补充说,"我们还不能讨论具体的时间",这些动漫作品究竟何时能够在其他阅读器上呈现,这是公司与亚马逊签订的秘密协议的内容。

亚马逊公司拒绝就此作出评论。

一些很难获得出版商专属经营权的独立书店认为这样的做法对消费者不利。

"一个竞争型的零售市场可以让消费者在不同的地方获得产品,创造更多的机会,营造一个竞争性的定价环境。"美国书商协会主席奥伦·泰歇尔说,"有选择总比没有选择好。"

不少读者也有同感。《睡魔》系列的作者尼尔·盖尔曼在他的博客中说,自从在"Twitter"上发布有关这次争端的微博之后,各种批评指责的信件蜂拥而至。其中一封这样写道:"当我听说《睡魔》将以电子书的形式上市时,我激动不已,但知道我和孩子们的阅读器无法获得这部漫画的电子书时,我的心碎了。"

盖尔曼表示直到亚马逊公司公布这一协议,他才得知这一消息,并对巴诺公司的行为做出批评。他在一封电子邮件中写道:"我的作品占所波及作品的12%。我不能理解巴诺公司对亚马逊公司获得数字专营权的反应,这实际上是同时把实体书专营权也拱手让给亚马逊公司及其他的独立书店,还为他们做了宣传。""不过从另一方面看,"他补充说,"他们也达到了目的,其他出版商以后在提供专属经营权之前将会三思而行。"

只有一群人在这场战争中似乎置身事外,隔岸观火,它们就是漫画书店。

"亚马逊与巴诺之间的斗争像一股浪潮,一次暴雨,或是一次地震,"位于加州伯克利的逃遁者漫画书店店主杰克·雷姆斯这样说:"对此我无能为力。"

然而有一件事例外。逃遁者漫画书店提供被两家连锁书店下架的漫画作品中的 20%。雷姆斯希望这份协议会给他带来更多的生意。

More to Read

  十几年前亚马逊公司成立时，只是一家新兴的图书销售网站。有人预计全美最大的书店巴诺书店将很快干掉它。而现实是，目前亚马逊书店比全球任何一家书店的存书要多 15 倍以上。而实现这一切既不需要庞大的建筑，又不需要众多的工作人员，亚马逊书店的 1600 名员工人均销售额 37.5 万美元，比全球最大的拥有 2.7 万名员工的巴诺图书公司要高 3 倍以上。今天亚马逊公司已经稳坐在线图书销售的头把交椅。传统实体书店在其冲击下丢盔弃甲，排名第二的边界连锁书店被迫关门大吉。巴诺书店不得不亦步亦趋地转向电子书销售及开发电子书阅读器。一方面，亚马逊公司与实体书店巨头的竞争愈演愈烈；另一方面，亚马逊公司又开始联合作者甩开出版社。据悉，亚马逊公司将出版 122 本各种体裁的书籍，提供印刷版和电子版两种版本。这也意味着亚马逊公司已经成功打通了从"作者"到"读者"的全部产业链，它将正式成为各大出版社的竞争对手，而这些出版商都曾是它最重要的供应商。有人说亚马逊公司真正的想法是，未来的图书出版只有 3 个环节，那就是作者、读者和亚马逊。可想而知，围绕电子书、围绕亚马逊，还会有更多的矛盾与纷争。

Reading Guidance

在"NBA"的历史上,有过无数光芒耀眼的巨星,但是只有一位被人们称为"篮球上帝",他身穿23号球衣,喜欢吐着舌头戏弄对手运球上篮,他1.98米的身高在长人如林的"NBA"赛场上显然是一个矮子,可只有他被称为"飞人"。他被公认为全世界最棒的篮球运动员,他不仅仅在其所处的那个时代,在整个NBA历史上都是最棒的——他就是迈克尔·乔丹。

Michael Jordan's 10 Secrets to Reaching the Top

Michael Jordan is the greatest basketball player that ever lived. Was he genetically predisposed to be faster and stronger, or was it his iron discipline that was responsible?

After completing my master's degree in Biomedical Science I can say, with some facts and knowledge to back it up, that genetics only partially added to the phenomenal talents of this outstanding athlete. He competed against people that were taller, stronger, faster, and younger than him. Despite the challenges he still came out on top.

Michael Jordan's 10 success secrets:

1. Take responsibility

"Some people want it to happen, some wish it would happen, others make it happen."

Throughout his life, Michael Jordan had the honorable quality of taking responsibility for his own destiny. That means that he took action while others paused to ask questions, gather more data, or consult experts. Not that he didn't have mentors, but essentially it was his wrists that snapped the ball into the hoop.

2. Give it a try

"I can accept failure, everyone fails at something. But I can't accept not trying."

One of the biggest causes of procrastination is the problem of hesitation. Sometimes people over think, and over analyze, which prevents them from taking that first step that will carry them one thousand miles. If you want to increase sales by trying a new technique, you will never know unless you try. This can apply to baking cakes, meeting singles, or anything that you can wrap your mind around.

3. Fail freely

"I've missed more than 9,000 shots in my career. I've lost almost 300 games. 26 times, I've been trusted to take the game winning shot and missed. I've failed over and over and over again in my life. And that is why I succeed."

Can you believe that Michael Jordan missed so many shots and lost so many games? I thought he was the best! Well, he is indeed the best, and it's because he was willing to fail, and keep going. That allowed him to get past his plateaus and persevere. That's another big reason for procrastination. When we think we'll fail, we do not attempt. A good solution is to consider what the worst case scenario of failing would be, because once you do that, it's never as bad as when the scenario was an unknown. Worst-case scenario is not that you'll die,

it's that you lived a miserable life as a coward.

4. Commit yourself

"The game is my wife. It demands loyalty and responsibility, and it gives me back fulfillment and peace."

Till death do we part, just me and my goal. I know in my heart that this is my role. When you give yourself fully and remove all other distractions you gain an invaluable level of attention to detail that will pool in resources you did not know you were capable of harnessing.

5. Enjoy your game

"Just play. Have fun. Enjoy the game."

So many people get stuck in dead end, zero-sum, no fun jobs because they didn't find their love, or just simply don't have the knack for taking pleasure in what they have. Consider the fact that you spend more time in your place of work than you do in your place of worship and with your family combined. By not being excited about, or getting full enjoyment out of work, you are cheating yourself from having a life of design and a life of fulfillment. I don't have a solution for your life, but I think you know which sacrifices you need to make, and are willing to make, in order to have the life of your dreams become your reality.

6. Play to win

"I play to win, whether during practice or a real game. And I will not let anything get in the way of me and my competitive enthusiasm to win."

Why bother playing the game of basketball, work, or life if you aren't planning to win? Do you even know what a statistically relevant way of measuring your personally defined "win" would look like? If you're in the game to make money does winning mean being the richest man in the world? If you're in the game for your family does that mean that you see them often and share the joys of life over a vibrant laugh? Whatever your game is, make sure you define what a win looks like, and play to win.

7. Be selfish and humble

"To be successful you have to be selfish, or else you never achieve. And once you get to your highest level, then you have to be unselfish. Stay reachable. Stay in touch. Don't isolate."

Take notes from Michael Jordan, first be selfish until you get on top, and once you are on top be humble and grounded. Being selfish in how you jump over people and slam dunk in their face, whether you are an athlete or business person. In a family setting this would mean taking care of your personal health before worrying about the well-being of your family. If you let your health fail you are of no use, or even worse a burden, to your family. This is why in case of an air plane emergency they tell you to put the air mask on yourself first and then on your children.

8. Find your way around

"Obstacles don't have to stop you. If you run into a wall, don't turn around and give up. Figure out how to climb it, go through it, or work around it."

Anything in life that is dear to us is worth so much because of the time and effort we put into acquiring it. One thing that determines how hard we've had to work is the amount of obstacles that were thrown in our way. Next time there's an obstacle, don't let it hinder you, think about the fact that whatever you're trying to reach will be that much worth it on the other side.

9. Make your own expectations

"If you accept the expectations of others, especially negative ones, then you never will change the outcome."

The number one thing that will literally ruin your life is if you live it by someone else's expectations. Every single person is different and has their own views on what's best, which follows what their goals are in this life. By listening to the voices of others, instead of your own voice, you are effectively submitting to live your life for the sake of accomplishing their goals. Set your own expecta-

tions, meet your own goals, and live your own extraordinary life.

10. Now, take one shot

"I never looked at the consequences of missing a big shot... when you think about the consequences you always think of a negative result."

The way this applies to life is quite simple. Much of the time we look too far into the future, while performing a task that needs our full attention right now. This act could take away our focus, paralyze us from taking action, and take away the pleasure of doing what is at hand. In life you can take one shot at a time, then another, and from this all your dreams will come true. At least that's what works for Michael Jordan.

Notes

predispose：使倾向于
mentor：导师，指导者
procrastination：耽搁，拖延
knack：技能，本领

迈克尔·乔丹攀上巅峰的十大秘诀

迈克尔·乔丹是迄今为止最伟大的篮球运动员。是因为他天生就比别人更敏捷、更强壮，还是应归因于他钢铁般的自律力？

我拿到生物医学的硕士学位后，掌握到一些事实和知识可以用来支持我的观点：遗传因素只是造就这位极具杰出才能的天才运动员的部分原

因。他与比他更高、更快、更年轻的运动员同场竞技,尽管充满挑战,他依然能独占鳌头。

迈克尔·乔丹的十大成功秘诀:

1. 担当责任

"一些人想要成功,一些人期盼成功,其他人努力行动获得成功。"

纵观迈克尔·乔丹的一生,他一直在坚持一种难能可贵的品质——为自己的使命、抱负担当责任。这意味着当其他人停下来质疑、收集更多资料或是询问专家时,他早已开始行动。不是因为他没有顾问,说到底是他用自己的手腕把球抓起并投进篮筐。

2. 勇于尝试

"我可以接受失败,因为每个人难免在某些事上经历失败。但是我无法接受不去尝试。"

造成拖延的最主要原因之一就是犹豫不决。有时候人们过度思考,过度分析,这会阻碍他们迈出第一步,而正是这一步可能让他们走到一千英里那么远。如果你想要通过新的技术来提高销量,除非你去尝试,不然你就绝不会知道这是否可行。同样的道理也适用于烤蛋糕、相亲或是任何会让你花费心思的事情。

3. 直面失败

"在我的篮球职业生涯中,我错失了9000多个投篮得分的机会。在几乎300场比赛中失利。整整26次,在别人相信我可以赢得那决定胜负的一分时,我却失误了。在我人生中,一次次地经历失败。这就是我成功的原因。"

你相信迈克尔·乔丹曾错失如此之多的得分机会,输过如此多场比赛吗?我认为他是最棒的!他的确是最棒、最好的,因为他直面失败,继续比赛。这让他走出低迷状态,依然故我,孜孜以求。害怕失败是造成拖延的另一个主要原因。当我们自认会失败时,常常不愿尝试。一个好的解决方法是设想一下失败会带来的最坏的结果,因为你一旦这样做,局面就不会如你面对未知结果时那么糟。最坏的结果不是死亡,而是像懦夫一样痛苦不堪地生活。

4. 全心投入

"比赛是我的妻子,她需要我的忠诚和责任,她也会给予我满足感和平和的心态。"

我和我的目标,相守百年。我深深知道这就是我的角色。当你全力付出,排除一切干扰,你就会具备极宝贵的一丝不苟的精神,这会给你带来超乎想象的掌控能力。

5. 享受比赛

"打球,快乐,享受比赛。"

很多人被困在没有前途、患得患失、乐趣全无的工作中,原因在于他们没有爱上自己的工作,或者只是缺少从所拥有的东西中获取快乐的本事。不妨考虑一下这个事实——你在工作上花的时间比你花在宗教和家庭这两者加起来的时间还多。不为工作而兴奋,不能从工作中得到愉悦,还声称自己享受着有计划又充实的生活,那是自欺欺人。我无法给你改变生活的良方,但如果你知道需要做出什么牺牲,也心甘情愿那样做,梦想与生活就会越走越近。

6. 争强好胜

"不管是训练还是比赛,我都争强好胜。我不会让任何事妨碍我和我对胜利的渴望。"

如果不想获胜,何必费力打篮球、工作或是生活?你是否知道如何以统计的方式,测量你个人界定的"赢"?如果你是为了钱去比赛,那么"赢"是否意味着成为世上最富有的人?如果你是为了家庭去比赛,那么"赢"是否意味着你可以常常和家人见面,一起在爽朗笑声中分享生活的乐趣?不管你的比赛是什么,先确定自己"赢"的含义,然后去比、去赢。

7. 自私自谦

"想成功就得自私,否则永远无法成功。一旦你到达了顶峰,你就必须做到不自私。不能高高在上、不可触及,也不要孤立自己。"

从迈克尔·乔丹所说的话来看,想要成功首先得自私,直到你攀上顶峰,一旦你到达顶峰你就要谦逊而踏实。不管你是一名运动员还是一位商人,当你越过别人,在他们面前灌篮时,所表现的是自私的一面。换位到家庭,这就意味着你在担心家人的健康前首先应顾及自己的身体健康。如果你身体不好,就对家庭毫无益处甚至成为家庭的负担。这就是为何在飞机遇到紧急情况时,机上的工作人员会告诉你先给自己戴上氧气面罩,然后才给孩子戴上。

8. 自谋出路

"障碍不一定会阻止你前进。如果你撞到一堵墙,不要转身走开,立即放弃。想想该如何去逾越、绕开,或是另辟蹊径。"

在生活中,那些我们所珍视的东西是因为我们为之投入的时间和精力才显得如此有价值。我们在行进路上所遇到的障碍,决定了我们努力的程度。下一次如果遇到障碍,别让它阻挡你,想想无论你试图获得什么,你的付出都是有价值的。

9. 自我期望

"如果你背负他人的期望,尤其是给你带来消极影响的期望,未来的结果可想而知。"

生活在他人的期望之下,这是真正毁掉你生活的罪魁祸首。每一个人都是与众不同的,对"最好的"以及"生活目标"有着各自的看法。如果只顾倾听他人的心声,却忽略自己的感受,你就会为达成他人的目标而委曲求全。制定你自己的期望,达成自己的目标,活出自己的精彩。

10. 积极行动

"我从不执著于错失得分的大好机会所产生的后果……当你想到这些,你总是会想坏的方面。"

这也适用于日常生活。很多时候我们忙于展望未来,往往忽略了完成手头任务所需要的全情投入。这样会使我们分散注意力,无法行动,也使我们丧失眼前工作中的乐趣。在生活中,每次投一个球,然后再投一个,你的梦想终将实现。至少对迈克尔·乔丹来说是这样的。

More to Read

乔丹的时代,也是"NBA"最辉煌的时代。乔丹对于篮球运动的巨大影响力不可避免地让人们把他推上了神坛。优雅、速度、力量、富有艺术性、即兴创造力和无比强烈的求胜欲望的完美结合——乔丹重新诠释了"超级巨星"的含义。与他相比,普通人的生活似乎平凡单调却不乏困扰,然而成功的背后必然隐藏着巨大的付出。现代社会各个领域都竞争激烈,更不用说人才济济的体育圈,如何突围,如何实现自身价值,如何得到他人认可,作者从迈克尔·乔丹的经历中总结出十条成功秘诀。乔丹不再只是高高在上的神话,他是我们生活里可以学习的榜样。

透视 PERCEPTION

Reading Guidance

　　本文作者是史蒂夫·保罗·乔布斯,常被人们昵称为史蒂夫·乔布斯(Steve Jobs),他就是我们所熟悉的苹果公司的创办人,世界公认的电脑业界的标志性和传奇性人物,也是美国创新精神的一面旗帜。2005 年 6 月 12 日,乔布斯在斯坦福大学的毕业典礼上作了这个题为"How to Live before You Die"的演讲。他在演讲中与莘莘学子分享了他的三个人生故事:如何把生命中的点点滴滴串联起来;关于爱和失去;死亡之事。本文节选的是其中最有名的第三个故事:死亡之事。文中出现的"Menlo Park"即门洛帕克市,位于美国加利福尼亚州圣马特奥县东南部。"毕业典礼"所对应的英文是"commencement","毕业典礼上的演讲"可以说成"commencement speech"或者"commencement address"。"commencement"的另外一个意思是"开始"。的确,毕业也即另一段人生旅程的开始。当我们站在人生的十字路口,即将左转或右行时,不妨读读这些文字,或许,它们能照亮我们的前程。

How to Live Before You Die

　　My third story is about death.
　　When I was 17, I read a quote that went something like: "If you live each day as if it was your last, someday you'll most certainly be right." It made an

impression on me, and since then, for the past 33 years, I have looked in the mirror every morning and asked myself: "If today were the last day of my life, would I want to do what I am about to do today?" And whenever the answer has been "No" for too many days in a row, I know I need to change something.

Remembering that I'll be dead soon is the most important tool I've ever encountered to help me make the big choices in life. Because almost everything—all external expectations, all pride, all fear of embarrassment or failure—these things just fall away in the face of death, leaving only what is truly important. Remembering that you are going to die is the best way I know to avoid the trap of thinking you have something to lose. You are already naked. There is no reason not to follow your heart.

About a year ago I was diagnosed with cancer. I had a scan at 7:30 in the morning, and it clearly showed a tumor on my pancreas. I didn't even know what a pancreas was. The doctors told me this was almost certainly a type of cancer that is incurable, and that I should expect to live no longer than three to six months. My doctor advised me to go home and get my affairs in order, which is doctor's code for prepare to die. It means to try to tell your kids everything you thought you'd have the next 10 years to tell them in just a few months. It means to make sure everything is buttoned up so that it will be as easy as possible for your family. It means to say your goodbyes.

I lived with that diagnosis all day. Later that evening I had a biopsy, where they stuck an endoscope down my throat, through my stomach and into my intestines, put a needle into my pancreas and got a few cells from the tumor. I was sedated, but my wife, who was there, told me that when they viewed the cells under a microscope the doctors started crying because it turned out to be a very rare form of pancreatic cancer that is curable with surgery. I had the surgery and I'm fine now.

This was the closest I've been to facing death, and I hope its the closest I get for a few more decades. Having lived through it, I can now say this to you with a bit more certainty than when death was a useful but purely intellectual concept:

No one wants to die. Even people who want to go to heaven don't want to die to get there. And yet death is the destination we all share. No one has ever escaped it. And that is as it should be, because death is very likely the single best invention of life. It is life's change agent. It clears out the old to make way for the new. Right now the new is you, but someday not too long from now, you will gradually become the old and be cleared away. Sorry to be so dramatic, but it is quite true.

Your time is limited, so don't waste it living someone else's life. Don't be trapped by dogma—which is living with the results of other people's thinking. Don't let the noise of others' opinions drown out your own inner voice. And most important, have the courage to follow your heart and intuition. They somehow already know what you truly want to become. Everything else is secondary.

When I was young, there was an amazing publication called *The Whole Earth Catalog*, which was one of the bibles of my generation. It was created by a fellow named Stewart Brand not far from here in Menlo Park, and he brought it to life with his poetic touch. This was in the late 1960's, before personal computers and desktop publishing, so it was all made with typewriters, scissors, and polaroid cameras. It was sort of like Google in paperback form, 35 years before Google came along: it was idealistic, and overflowing with neat tools and great notions.

Stewart and his team put out several issues of *The Whole Earth Catalog*, and then when it had run its course, they put out a final issue. It was the mid-1970s, and I was your age. On the back cover of their final issue was a photograph of an early morning country road, the kind you might find yourself hitchhiking on if you were so adventurous. Beneath were the words: "Stay Hungry. Stay Foolish." It was their farewell message as they signed off. Stay Hungry. Stay Foolish. And I have always wished that for myself. And now, as you grad-

uate to begin anew, I wish that for you.

Stay Hungry. Stay Foolish.

Notes

pancreas：胰脏
sedated：镇静的
destination：目的地
intuition：直觉

我生未竟，精彩不断

第三个故事是"死亡之事"。

我17岁那年，读到了一句话："如果你把每一天都当做生命中最后一天去生活的话，那么有一天你会发现自己是正确的。"这句话给我留下了深刻的印象。从那时开始，过了33年，我在每天早晨都会对着镜子问自己："如果今天是我生命中的最后一天，你会不会完成你今天想做的事情呢？"当答案连续多天是"不"的时候，我知道自己需要改变某些事情了。

"记住你即将死去"是我一生中遇到的最重要的箴言，它帮我做出了生命中重要的选择。因为几乎所有的事情——所有的荣誉、所有的骄傲、所有对难堪和失败的恐惧——都会在死亡面前烟消云散，留下来的是你生命中最重要的事情。有时候你会担心自己将失去某些东西，"记住你即将死去"是我知道的避免这些想法的最好办法。你已经赤身裸体了，你没有理由不去跟随自己内心的声音。

透视 PERCEPTION

大概一年以前,我被诊断出癌症。我在早晨7点半做了一个检查,检查结果清楚地显示我的胰腺里长了个肿瘤。我当时都不知道胰腺是干什么的。医生告诉我那很可能是一种无法治愈的癌症,我还有三到六个月的时间活在这个世界上。我的医生叫我回家,整理好自己的一切,那是医生面对临终病人时的标准程序。那意味着你将要把未来十年要对自己孩子说的话在几个月里全都说完;那意味着你要把每件事情都安排好,让你的家人尽可能轻松地生活下去;那也意味着说"再见"的时候到了。

我拿着那个诊断书待了一整天,那天晚上我做了一个活体切片检查,医生将一个内窥镜从我的喉咙伸进去,经过胃,再进入肠子,然后用一根针在我的胰腺肿瘤上取了几个细胞。我当时是被麻醉的,但是我的妻子在那里。她后来告诉我,当医生在显微镜下观察这些细胞的时候他们开始尖叫,因为这些细胞竟然是一种非常罕见的可以用手术来治愈的胰腺癌症细胞。之后我做了这个手术,现在我痊愈了。

那是我最接近死亡的时候,我希望这也是以后的几十年最接近死亡的一次。从死亡线上又活了过来,我可以比以前把死亡当成一种想象中的概念的时候,更为肯定地对你们说:

没有人愿意死,即使人们想上天堂,也不会为了去那里而死。但是死亡是我们每个人共同的归宿。从来没有人能够逃脱死亡。也应该如此。因为死亡就是生命中最好的一个发明。它破旧立新,将旧的清除以便给新的让路。你们现在是新的,但是从现在开始,不久以后,你们将会逐渐变成旧的,然后被送离人生舞台。我很抱歉,这虽然很有戏剧性,但却是千真万确的。

你们的时间很有限,所以不要将它们浪费在重复其他人的生活上。不要被教条束缚,那意味着你要和其他人思考的结果一起生活。不要让其他人喧嚣的观点掩盖你内心真正的声音。此外,最重要的是,你要有勇气去听从你直觉和心灵的指示——它们在某种程度上更知道你想要成为什么样子,而其他所有的事情都是次要的。

当我年轻的时候,有一本名为《地球目录》的杂志,很发人深省,它是我们那一代人的圣经之一。它是一个叫斯图尔特·布兰迪的家伙在离这里

〈103〉

不远的门洛帕克编辑的,他像诗人一般神奇地将这本杂志带到了这个世界。那是20世纪60年代后期,个人电脑即将诞生的前夕。所以,这本书全部是用打字机、剪刀还有偏光镜所打造的。它很类似于我们今天的谷歌,只不过它是软皮包装的。在谷歌出现35年之前:这是理想主义的,其中有许多灵巧的工具和伟大的想法。

斯图尔特和他的伙伴出版了几期的《地球目录》,当它完成了自己使命的时候,他们做出了最后一期的目录。那是在20世纪70年代的中期,我正处在你们现在这个年纪。在最后一期杂志的封底上印的是清晨乡村公路的照片(如果你有冒险精神的话,你可以自己找到这条路的),在照片下面有这样一段话:"求知若饥,虚心若愚。"这是他们停刊时的告别语。"求知若饥,虚心若愚。"我总是希望自己能够那样做,现在,在你们即将毕业,开始新的旅程的时候,我也希望你们能做到这一点。

求知若饥,虚心若愚。

More to Read

乔布斯是佛教徒、素食主义者,招牌打扮是黑T恤加牛仔裤。不过此前,他可不是这样的打扮。当时的他最喜欢的是领结。从装扮的改变上可以看出乔布斯在内心上的返璞归真。2011年8月25日,乔布斯宣布辞去苹果CEO的职务,舆论一片哗然。2011年10月6日,乔布斯悄然离世,全世界无数"果粉"黯然神伤,以各种方式去纪念他们心目中的"神"。乔布斯真诚地告诉我们,要把每一天当成生命的最后一天,而他自己也全心全意地践行着这一信条。

透 视 PERCEPTION

Reading Guidance

  本文作者约瑟夫·雷诺德将写日记的好处娓娓道来。他写日记的经历很能引起读者的共鸣。作者在文章中提到了不少重量级的文化名人,在这里为读者作以简单的介绍,希望有助于大家理解文章的妙处。塞缪尔·约翰逊(Samuel Johnson)是18世纪英国最重要的作家之一,在英国人心目中有着难以取代的地位。他一生著述甚丰,但最有影响的却是完成于1755年的两卷本《英语词典》(*The Dictionary of the English Language*)。在长达150年的时间里,这本词典一直是最权威的英语词典,直到20世纪初才被《牛津英语词典》取代。亨利·大卫·梭罗(Henry David Thoreau)是美国作家、哲学家,著有散文集《瓦尔登湖》和论文《论公民的不服从权利》。梭罗对美国文明的独立发展有不可估量的影响力。埃尔文·布鲁克斯·怀特(E. B. White)是美国当代著名散文家、评论家,以散文闻名,"其文风冷峻清丽,辛辣幽默,自成一格"。怀特是《纽约客》的主要撰稿人之一,奠定了影响深远的"《纽约客》文风"。他还写了三本经典儿童读物:《精灵鼠小弟》、《夏洛的网》与《吹小号的天鹅》。

I Think (and Write in a Journal), Therefore I Am

  "I write, therefore I am," wrote Samuel Johnson, altering Descartes' fa-

mous dictum: "I think, therefore I am."

When writing in my journal, I feel keenly alive and somehow get a glimpse of what Johnson meant.

My journal is a storehouse, a treasury for everything in my daily life: the stories I hear, the people I meet, the quotations I like... Unless I capture these things in writing, I lose them.

All writers are such collectors, whether they keep a journal or not; they see life clearly, a vision we only recognize when reading their books, Thoreau exemplifies the best in journal writing—his celebrated *Walden* grew out of his journal entries.

By writing in my own journal, I often make discoveries. I see connections and conclusions that otherwise would not appear obvious to me. I become a craftsman, like a potter or a carpenter who makes a vase or a wooden stoop out of parts. Writing is a source of pleasure when it involves such invention and creation.

I want to work on my writing, too hone it into clear, readable prose, and where better to practice my writing than in my journal. Writing, I'm told, is a skill, and improves with practice. I secretly harbor this hope. So my journal becomes the area where I do battle with the written word.

Sometimes when I have nothing to write, I sit idly and thumb back through old entries. I rediscover incidents long forgotten.

During a recent cold midwinter night, for example, I reread an entry dated a summer ago. My wife and I had just returned after a long ride home, but our spirits were lifted when we saw our cat come down the driveway to greet us, her tail held high shouting her presence. By reading this entry, I relived the incident, warming with affection for my cat and a sunny day at the beach.

I always try to write something, however, even if it is free writing, writing anything that comes into mind. Often this process is a source of a "core idea" tat can later be developed into a more finely polished piece of writing.

透视 PERCEPTION

Journal writing, in addition, is a time when I need not worry about the rules of spelling and grammar; it provides a relaxed atmosphere in which my ideas and feelings can flow freely onto the page. If I discover an idea worth developing, then my prewriting is done.

My journal becomes a place where I can try different kinds of writing, as well, from prose and poetry to letters to the editor. Attempting different kinds is useful; once I find the inspiring medium, my writing improves.

When I write in my journal, I seek the solitude of my study. With pen in hand, I become omniscient; I am aware of the quiet, damp, night air, or the early-mooring sounds of life.

"Usually when a man quits writing in his journal, he has lost interest in life," attests E. B. White, and inveterate journal writer himself.

So for these few moments, at least, I hold myself in hand, I am.

....

Notes

celebrated:著名的
idly:懒散地

我思、我写，故我在

塞缪尔·约翰逊曾经效仿笛卡尔的名言"我思故我在"说"我写故我在"。

当我在写日记的时候，能真切地感觉到自己的存在，因此也对约翰逊

〈107〉

的说法心有戚戚。

我的日记无异于一座宝库，收藏着我平日生活的点点滴滴：我道听途说的轶事，我遇见的那些人，我喜欢的语录……如果我不把它们一一写下来，就都忘掉了。

作家也是收藏家，不论是否写日记，他们都能洞察生活，而我们只有品读他们的作品时才能体会到这些不同寻常的见地。梭罗在写日记方面堪称典范——他著名的《瓦尔登湖》就源于他的日记。

我在写日记时也时常有些新发现。很多平时不甚明晰的关系与结论居然在写日记时能够看得很清楚了。同时，我也变成了一个匠人，就像制作花瓶的陶工或者木凳的木匠一般。因为写日记也离不开发明与创造，这成了我快乐的源泉。

我也想在写作上有些建树，把我平时记录所得润色为清新、可读的散文随笔，毕竟这种文体比写日记更能锤炼文笔。有人说，写作是一种技巧，熟能生巧。我其实是有这种小"私心"的。所以，日记就是我字斟句酌、遣词造句的一方舞台。

我也有无事可记的时候。于是，我就静静地翻看曾经的那些记录，遗忘许久的事情忽又历历在目了。

近来，在一个寒冷的冬夜，我重温了去年夏天的一篇日记。那时，我和妻子刚从海边度假归来。我们风尘仆仆开车回家，一路舟车劳顿让我们疲惫不堪，但是当我们看到我们的爱猫在车道上迎接我们时，一下子就来了精神，猫咪的尾巴翘得高高的，喵喵地叫，提醒我们它在这里。当我读到这篇日记时，美好的记忆涌上心头，对猫咪的喜爱之情，记忆中那个充满阳光的海滩，让我浑身暖意洋洋。

我时常拿起笔写点东西，天马行空，想到哪就写到哪。而这些零散的文字又成为日后某篇好文章的"内核"。

此外，写日记时，我无须担心拼写和语法规则，在这样轻松的氛围中，我的思想感情便能够自由地跃然纸上。每每有值得一写的想法时，我就预先写在日记中，以待后用。

从散文诗歌到写给编辑的书信，我都先写在日记中，它成了我尝试不同文体的园地。这对我非常有好处,它极大地鼓舞了我写作的热情,而我的写作水平也日渐提高。

当我写日记时,书房是那么宁静。一笔在手,我便思接千古,神游八荒;静谧而潮润的夜晚的空气或者清晨的天籁都是那般切近。是的,在写日记时,我越发走近了生活。

埃尔文·布鲁克斯·怀特是写日记的高手,他曾经说:"如果一个人不写日记,他便丧失了对生活的兴趣。"

的确,在日记中,我是掌握在我自己手中的,哪怕只是片刻,我毕竟还存在着。

More to Read

其实现代人对写日记是非常痴迷和在行的,只不过形式"进化"了很多。在互联网时代,我们写日记的工具从简单的纸笔进化为电脑屏幕、键盘甚至是手写笔。日记也随之衍生出很多新的变体,比如博客(blog)、微博(microblog)等等。大家在网络中不断查看别人的日志,遇到好的内容就进行转载,时时更新自己的日志。柴米油盐、国家大事、阳春白雪、下里巴人,通通被写进了日记。有了现代日记的网络变得异常活跃,生活变得事无巨细。以前,写日记是个人的私密行为,把日记本锁在抽屉的小角落,细心呵护,生怕被人发现了内心的秘密。现在,我们喜欢晒日记,而且乐此不疲。日记真要是写好了,说不定还会积攒起一群粉丝呢!约瑟夫·雷诺德看到日记的进化会不会惊呼"这世界变化快"呢?然而,变的只是日记的形式而已。归根结底,"在写日记时,我越发走进了生活。"

Reading Guidance

哈佛最受本科生欢迎的选修课是"幸福课",场面很火爆,俨然已经成为美国大学校园文化的一道风景线。教这门课的是一位名不见经传的年轻教师——泰勒·本—沙哈尔。据他自己说,他性格内向,比较害羞,"我曾不快乐了30年"。本—沙哈尔毕业于哈佛大学,而且从本科一直读到博士。他曾是哈佛大学三名优秀生之一,并被派往剑桥大学进行交流。此外,他在运动和社团活动方面也很积极。但这些外在的光环未能让他感到幸福快乐。他曾说,自己的内心并不快乐,"最初,引起我对积极心理学兴趣的是我的经历。我开始意识到,与外在的东西相比,内在的东西对产生幸福感所起的作用更大。通过研究这门学科,我受益匪浅。我想把我所学的东西和别人分享,于是,我决定做一名教师。"另外,文中提到的常春藤联盟(the Ivy League)指的是美国八所顶尖的私立大学:哈佛大学、哥伦比亚大学、耶鲁大学、康奈尔大学、宾夕法尼亚大学、普林斯顿大学、布朗大学、达特茅斯学院。

They Teach Happiness at Harvard

In Tal Ben-Shahar's positive psychology class, students learn that happiness isn't just an accident; it's a science.

An entire industry has been built up around the pursuit of happiness. A stroll past any bookstore window demonstrates the explosive popularity of the feel-good, self-help movements of recent years. And whether these products are genuine paths to ultimate happiness or just pleasure-peddling scams, the trend seems likely to hold.

Now, even the Ivy League is getting in on the act, layering serious academic research onto the pop-psychology phenomenon to develop a "science of happiness". Known as "positive psychology", the field was pioneered at the University of Pennsylvania and came to Harvard a decade ago when an elective course on the topic was first taught.

Since then, Positive Psychology has become the most popular undergraduate course at Harvard, eclipsing the previous longtime title holder, Introduction to Economics. The success of the course, which focuses on the psychological aspects of a fulfilling and flourishing life, indicates a growing desire by young people to make their lives more meaningful, says Tal Ben-Shahar, a Harvard psychologist who has taught the class since 2004.

"Students are attracted to this kind of class because they feel that it's making a real difference in their lives," says Ben-Shahar, whose charismatic personality and compelling lectures helped drive explosive growth in enrollment after he began teaching the course. Ben-Shahar says the quest for happiness has always been an innate human yearning, dating back to the times of Confucius and Aristotle. "The difference today is that for the first time we have a science of happiness."

To be sure, the course has its doubters. James Coyne, a psychologist and researcher at the University of Pennsylvania School of Medicine says that Harvard's class and others like it offer little more to increase happiness than does a motivational speaker on a lecture circuit. The sense of euphoric bliss after a compelling presentation is natural, he says, but rarely lasts. "People always readjust to their baseline and go back to normal," says Coyne.

But the point of Positive Psychology is to combine the fun of popular psychology with academic rigor. The course's syllabus reads like a 12-step recovery pro-

gram with lesson titles such as "Can We Change?" "Setting Goals", "Relationships", and "Self-Esteem". But the list of course readings dispels any notion that the class is what Harvard students call a "gut", or easy credit. Articles, essays, and research reports from vaunted science publications like the journal of *Cognitive Psychotherapy* and *Psychology Today* are juxtaposed with Ben-Shahar's own book on the subject, *Happier: Learn the Secrets to Daily Joy and Lasting Fulfillment*.

Despite the heavy workload, the popularity of Positive Psychology has soared. In 2006, more than 850 students filed into the auditorium for the semester's first lesson, up from just 20 in 1999 when the course was launched. Many credit the class's success to Ben-Shahar himself, whose on-campus popularity coupled with media attention has made him a quasi-celebrity in the field of psychology. (He even appeared on *The Daily Show* with Jon Stewart in 2007.) But Ben-Shahar insists it's the science that is the real draw.

Elizabeth Johnston, who was in Ben-Shahar's section in 2004, began the course with skepticism. "I was one of the naysayers," she recalls. "I said this is crazy, I can't believe this; I want a real psychology class." But as the semester progressed, Johnston says she became a believer. She was fascinated partly by the course literature and message, and partly by Ben-Shahar's colorful personal anecdotes, which she says were inspirational.

Before taking Positive Psychology, Johnston was obsessed with grades and focused completely on her future. She says the class taught her to enjoy living for the moment and to express gratitude more openly, among other things. "A lot of people think positive psychology means walking around with a smile on your face," says Johnston, who went on to earn a master's degree in positive psychology at the University of Pennsylvania. "It's not that. It's learning to take the good with the bad and learning to make the most of your life."

The phenomenon of positive psychology appears to be catching on. Today, more than 200 courses on the subject are taught across the U.S. and Ben-Shahar has given seminars about it as far away as China. "The role of a university is ultimately to improve the quality of people's lives," he says, adding that that is precisely what positive psychology is intended to do.

....

Notes

  scam：骗局

  flourishing：繁荣的，昌盛的，欣欣向荣的

  enrollment：登记，注册

  baseline：底线

  juxtapose：并列

  anecdote：逸闻趣事

哈佛的幸福人生

  在泰勒·本—沙哈尔的积极心理学课上，学生们懂得了幸福不是一次偶然，而是一门科学。

  追求幸福俨然已经成为一个产业，蔚为壮观。随便在大大小小的书店逛上一圈，便会发现近些年流行起来的"我要幸福"、"自救、自励"的运动是多么的深入人心，书店的橱窗已经成为相关书籍的天下。且不论这些产品是否能够真正引领我们走向幸福，是否只是些哗众取宠、兜售快乐的骗局，这个运动似乎已经非常深入人心了。

  现在，连常春藤联盟也开始涉足其中了。它们的加盟为这个大众心理学现象罩上了一层学术的面纱，并将之发展为"幸福科学"——"积极心理学"。这个领域是由常春藤联盟中的宾夕法尼亚大学开创的，十年后传播

至哈佛大学。那时,哈佛大学开设了一门关于积极心理学的选修课。

自此,积极心理学成为哈佛大学本科生的热门课,甚至还让以前有"选课王"美誉的经济学导论黯然失色。泰勒·本—沙哈尔是哈佛大学的心理学家,他从 2004 年开始教授这门课。他说,积极心理学这门课主要是从心理学的角度来阐释如何获得愉快丰盈的人生,它的成功也暗示了年轻人对于人生价值与意义的迫切渴望和追求。

本—沙哈尔说:"学生们之所以对这类课趋之若鹜,是因为他们想要为自己的人生带来些改变。"本—沙哈尔讲授这门课后,他本人非凡的人格魅力和让人为之动容的讲座迅速提高了该课的人气,学生们竞相选修该课。本—沙哈尔说,对于幸福的追求源自人的本性,无论是孔子还是亚里士多德都叩问过这个问题。"所不同的是,我们今天首次提出了幸福科学这个说法。"

当然,这门课也不乏质疑者,比如詹姆士·科恩尼。他是宾夕法尼亚大学医学院的心理学家和研究人员。他说,比起那些在大学讲坛上做讲座的演讲者,哈佛的幸福课和其他类似的课程并不能更为有效地提升学生们的幸福感。他还说,学生们在一堂激动人心的幸福课后,感觉到兴奋欣喜,这是很自然的事情,但是这种感觉并不会持久。"人们总是习惯于按照自己的底线进行自我调整,然后再归于正常。"

但是,积极心理学的意义在于,它将大众心理学的娱乐性与学术精神融为一体。这门课的课程安排就像是 12 步走的恢复性计划一样,包括名为"我们能获得改变吗?""确立目标""关系""自尊"这样的讲座。但是这门课的阅读书单却很吓人,绝不是一门好拿学分的课程。学生们既要阅读《认知心理学》等大有来头的学术期刊上的文章、论文、研究报告,还要学习本—沙哈尔自己的著作——《再幸福些:日常快乐和持久幸福的秘诀》。

尽管学习负担很重,可是积极心理学这门课却越来越受欢迎。2006 年,近 900 人到礼堂去聆听第一学期的第一堂幸福课。1999 年,在这门课开课之初,只有 20 人选修。很多人将这门课的成功归功于本—沙哈尔本人。他在校园的人气加之媒体的关注使其成为心理学界的大腕。(2007 年,他甚至出现在了约翰·斯图尔特主持的《每日秀》中。)但是本—沙哈尔坚称真正富有魅力的是幸福科学本身。

透视 PERCEPTION

伊丽莎白·约翰逊于2004年选修了本—沙哈尔的幸福课,起初她还是将信将疑。"我是其中的一个怀疑者。"她回忆道:"我说这简直是疯了,我才不信呢,我要的是一个真正的心理学课。"但是,随着学习的深入,她还是相信了。她为课堂上的文献和信息着迷,也为本—沙哈尔多姿多彩、鼓舞人心的个人经历着迷。

在选修积极心理学这门课前,约翰逊最看重的是成绩,把全部的重点都放在对于未来的规划上。她说这门课教会了她如何享受当下,如何真心地表达感激之情,很多很多。毕业后,约翰逊来到了宾夕法尼亚大学攻读积极心理学硕士学位。她说:"很多人都认为积极心理学是在教人如何面带微笑地生活。但其实不是。它的目的在于教会我们人生不论好坏,都要照单全收,要学着充分享受我们的人生。"

积极心理学现象好像还在持续升温。今天,全美有200多个与积极心理学相关的课程,可谓门类繁多。本—沙哈尔甚至远赴中国进行讲学。正如他所言:"大学的终极使命是提高人类的生活质量。"这也正是积极心理学所致力研究的。

More to Read

正如泰勒·本—沙哈尔所说,对于幸福的追求是人的天性。当我们的物质财富积累达到一定程度时,便自然而然地关注起"幸福",因为我们发现一味增加的物质财富并不能给予我们更多的幸福。于是,我们开始寻找令自己幸福起来的良方,有的人归隐田园,有的人散尽钱财搞慈善,有的人环游世界,还有的人研究积极心理学,努力地修身养性。其实,越是在经济高速发展的时代,人们越关注幸福指数,哈佛大学积极心理学的火爆,中国学者对于孔子哲学的反思与解读都证明了这一点。人生的意义和价值何在?这不仅是让哈佛学生困惑的问题,中国的大学生又何尝不在追问这个问题。但愿有一天中国的大学也能为学生们开设出这样精彩的选修课,让他们明白成功不是人生的唯一追求,生活的苦与乐,笑和泪都应照单全收。这就是生活!

Reading Guidance

"火人节"（Burning Man）是由一个名为"黑岩城"（Black Rock City, LLC）的组织发起的反传统的狂欢节，为期8天。自1986年开创以来，年年举行，举办地选在美国内华达州黑岩沙漠（Black Rock Desert，位于里诺市东北方向150千米处）。时间一般选在为8月底到9月初的美国劳工节。近年来，参与者人数不断攀升。所有的参与者都有一个非常好玩的称呼"火人"（Burner）。来自世界各地的"火人"每年都相聚在寸草不生的荒漠里，借由想象建起一个寿命只用8天的临时城市。厕所是城中唯一的现代设施。"火人"们能买到的只有冰和咖啡。其他所有生活用品均须自带。8天过后，"火人"们"不留一丝痕迹"（leave no trace）地离开，所有垃圾都得自己打包带走，就好像根本不曾有人来过一样。火人节以集异想天开与荒诞之大成而著称，一切奇事都汇集到这个沙漠中的狂热节日中，每年都有大批标榜自由的年轻人到此以激进的方式"表现自己"。

Burning Man: Puts Other Festivals in the Shade

In late 1986, a beach party celebrating the summer solstice marked the first official Burning Man. Within a few years, its participants had become so many, and its activities so outlandish, that founder Larry Harvey and his friends decided to move the festival to somewhere more appropriate. They chose the Black Rock Desert, a 100-mile prehistoric lakebed in north-western Nevada, where temperatures regularly reach 110°F.

By 1997, Burning Man was already well on the way to becoming a cultural phenomenon. That year 10,000 people turned up to experience a week of desert living, far outside the mainstream culture of the United States. Within "Black Rock City", participants abide by a gift economy, in which commerce of any type is expressly forbidden. "Burners" must bring all their own food, camping equipment and water; and are expected to "participate" in one form or another. Many choose to construct extraordinary temporal pieces of art: full size buildings made of driftwood and junk, flashing sculptures belching flames into the night. Walking around the desert after dark, this formerly empty expanse shimmers with a thousand projections and creations, impromptu performances, DJ booths, fantastical art cars resembling pirate ships and dragonflies. "It's like stepping through the looking glass," one Burner told me. "The default world—which is what we call the world outside—just can't compare with this."

In 2007, numbers at Burning Man reached 35,000. There were people of every age group, from every stratum of society. I was among them, knowing no one, expecting little more than a fun week in a somewhat surreal environment. And yet, like thousands before me, the week was transformative, life changing, instantly addictive. This third largest city in Nevada (vanishing "without a trace" after the festival) was spotlessly clean, full of highly creative and considerate individuals. People travelled everywhere by bicycle, some of them naked. Everywhere I went, people offered me food, free rides on their "mutant vehicles", invitations to all-night parties, yoga lessons. Dressed in bizarre costumes, wearing sand goggles and dust masks, it seemed easy to take people at face value, little caring what they did outside Black Rock. The annual theme, which last year was entitled Green Man, seemed to perfectly mesh with the zeitgeist. Invention and great creativity was needed to rethink the carbon-based

structure of our world. At Burning Man that world seemed to rise up in the present moment, ecologically sound and full of laughter.

It would be all to easy to write off Burning Man as a desert rave, a 21st-century update on Woodstock. But more than any of those things, Burning Man is a philosophy, an attempt to reinvent the parameters and constraints of society. Within the most advanced capitalist economy in the world, participants choose to free themselves from commerce. Art works are anonymous, often destroyed at the end of the week, even in the case of colossal structures taking months to build. People make an effort to help each other—a necessary step, actually, given the potentially hostile natural environment. Unlike any other festival I've visited, it's one without celebrity, corporate logos, or personal egos of any kind.

"Given the current cultural and political climate in the United States," Geoffrey told me, a veteran Burner of seven years, "this is really the only sane place left. I've been incredibly broke this year and wasn't sure I was going to make it, but then I realized that I had to be here, it's the only truly sacred experience open to me right now."

Perhaps more even than the enlightening effects of doing without money, running water or cell phone connection, Burning Man seems to effect a spiritual magnetism on those who attend. From above, the circular design of the city, carefully zoned each year, seems akin to some ancient pagan site. With its fire worship, close connection to nature, and emphasis on participation, Burning Man offers a transcendent experience to all comers. Each year, a Temple of Forgiveness invites people to inscribe the names of loved ones who have passed away on its walls and ceilings, before the whole structure goes up in flames, in a grand gesture of emancipation.

For myself, as I rode my bicycle far out on to the prehistoric lakebed at midnight, looking backwards on the glittering utopia that is Black Rock City, Burning Man seemed like the freest place on earth. Behind me, people from all

透视 PERCEPTION

over the world were gathered in what felt like some kind of non-denominational worship. I wasn't exactly sure what we were worshipping, but it felt significant. Significant enough that back in the "default" world, my first act was to book my ticket for 2008.

Notes

outlandish：古怪的,奇异的
stratum：岩层,层
transcendent：卓越的,至高无上的

妙趣横生——火人节

火人节是以 1986 年在海边举行的一个庆祝夏至的派对为诞生标志的。几年时间中,参加者迅速增加,活动也变得光怪陆离,创立者拉里·哈维和他的朋友们不得不决定把节日的庆祝地点改在更为合适的偏僻地方。他们最后选定了黑岩沙漠,那是一个史前河床,有 100 英里宽,在内华达州东北部,常温都在华氏 110 度左右。

到了 1997 年,火人节已经成为一种文化现象了。那一年,有 1 万人去体验这种为期一个礼拜、与美国主流文化生活大相径庭的沙漠生活。参加节日的人们生活在一种"赠送"经济体制之下,任何买卖行为都是明令禁止的。"火人"(参加火人节的人)必须自带食物、设备和水,并且以某种形式参与到"分配"中去。很多人还会制作一些即时而又特别的艺术品:用各种废品制作的与实物比例为一比一的建筑物、夜明雕塑等。天黑后漫步在沙

漠之中，曾经空旷的区域被闪闪发光的作品、即兴演出、音乐棚、装扮成海盗船或大蜻蜓的汽车等填满。"我感觉好像走进了窥镜一样，"一个火人说，"残缺的世界（指外部世界）根本没法与之媲美。"

2007年，参加火人节的人数达到了3.5万人，他们来自社会各个阶层，男女老少都有。我也是其中的一员，这里没有我认识的人，但我还是盼望着能在这个超现实主义环境中度过有趣的一个星期。和其他人一样，这不同以往的一周简直让我分外着迷。这个内华达州第三大的城市（节日过后就会消失得无影无踪）一尘不染，居民们都具有很高的创造力，并且做事细心周到。人们出行都骑着自行车，有些喜欢裸体。每到一处，都有人给我提供食物，还可以免费搭乘经过他们改装的交通工具，我还被邀请参加午夜派对，体验瑜伽课程。穿着怪异的服装，带着太阳镜和防尘面具，你只需要关注人们在这里的表现，完全不用考虑他们在黑岩城外面的行为。火人节每年都有一个主题，去年的主题"绿人"非常符合时代精神。我们该重新考虑一下这个以碳为基础的世界，然后再去搞发明创造。火人节的世界超越了外部世界，生态和谐，充满欢笑。

可以简单地把火人节当成一场"沙漠风暴"，或者21世纪更新版的伍德斯托克音乐节。但是火人节更是一种哲学，一种试图重新定义和约束社会的努力。在世界上最发达的资本主义国家，人们却选择从商业中解放出来。那些艺术作品通常是匿名的，即使是那些花上几个月完成的庞大建筑，在活动结束时都会被一并销毁。使人们努力互相帮助的必要条件是处于恶劣的环境之中。和我参加的其他节日不同，这个节日没有名人、社团标识或者任何形式的利己主义行为。

杰弗里，一个参加过七届火人节的人告诉我说："在美国当前的文化和政治氛围中，这里是唯一的一片净土。本来我以为我今年伤势太严重，无法去参加了。但是不久我就认识到一点，那就是我必须得到那里去。因为那是目前唯一能让我体验到圣洁的地方。"

人们对火人节的痴迷也许并不只限于体验没有钞票、自来水和手机的生活，火人节有其精神引力。首先，城市的环状设计、每年都精心划分的不同区域，酷似古代的宗异教遗址。对火的崇拜就把人们与大自然紧密联系起来,同时又向人们强调分享的重要性。火人节还能给所有参与者一种超自然的神秘感。每年都会有一座"宽恕之塔"在庄严的气氛中被烧掉,以祈祷那些逝去的但还有人爱着的人们得到宽恕,他们的名字就写在塔上。在塔燃烧起来之前,主办人会邀请参与者记住那些人的名字。

  我是在午夜骑着车离开这个史前河床的。离开时我不时恋恋不舍地回头看这个光芒闪烁的乌托邦,想着这里应该是这个世界上最自由的地方了吧。在我身后,世界各地的人们聚集在一起,没有任何宗教崇拜的意味。我不能肯定我们到底崇拜着什么,但是却感觉到这种崇拜的重要性。它重要得让我觉得,我回到残缺的世界的第一件事就是给自己预订2008年火人节的门票。

More to Read

  美国大众文化的一个很不容忽视或者很令人羡慕的地方就是"DIY"(do-it-yourself)。从供孩子玩耍的小树屋到小家具,他们都愿意自己尝试着动手去做。再看看美国的节日,俨然就是美国人大秀"DIY"技巧的舞台。万圣节时,人们会自己做可怕的行头;圣诞节时,他们亲手将圣诞树装扮得漂漂亮亮;复活节时,大人、孩子都以画彩蛋为乐。难怪,大家都说美国人很有创意。创意的火花都源自于日常生活的点滴积累。手巧,则心灵。本文中所介绍的火人节无疑又从另一个侧面反映了美国人的"DIY"精神。在自给自足,没有商品交换的沙漠中,人们返璞归真,与自然亲密接触。要想生存下去,必须自己动手。此外,火人节也传达了人们的环保理念,狂欢过后,一切都恢复如常,没有生活垃圾,没有临时搭建的房屋。真的应了徐志摩的那句诗:"悄悄的我走了,正如我悄悄的来,我挥一挥衣袖,不带走一片云彩。"

Reading Guidance

本文作者是艾伦·古德曼。1963年,刚刚大学毕业的古德曼就职于《新闻周刊》(Newsweek),当时美国的新闻界仍是男人的天下,所以初出茅庐的她只能从一名普通的研究人员做起,而无缘写作。后来,她来到波士顿,开始为《波士顿环球报》(The Boston Globe)写专栏。通过这个专栏,她的名字逐渐为人所知。古德曼写了很多有影响的文章。1980年,她凭借出色的评论文章而将美国新闻界的最高奖项普利策奖收入囊中。她还出版了五部专栏文集:《近乡》(Close to Home)、《细说》(At Large)、《保持联络》(Keeping in Touch)、《有理》(Making Sense)和《文字之路》(Paper Trail)。作为女性,古德曼在她的著作《转折点》(Turning Points)和《我明白你的意思:女性生活中友谊的力量》(I Know Just What You Mean: The Power of Friendship in Women's Lives)中表达了她对女性成长与生活的关注。在本文中,美丽的蝴蝶引发了作者对生活的重新思考。

Learning to Brake for Butterflies

Casco Bay, Maine—I arrive here coasting on the fumes of hi-octane anxiety. The split-second timing of my daily life has adhered to my mood like a watch strapped to a wrist.

透视 PERCEPTION

Behind me is a deadline met by the skin of my teeth. A plane was late. A gas tank was empty. A boat was missed.

The carry-on baggage of my workaday life has accompanied me onto the island. An L. L. Bean bag full of work, a fax machine, a laptop with a modem. I have all sorts of attachments to the great new machine that feeds me its fast-food through the electronic stomach tube.

Fully equipped this way, I tell myself that I can get an extra week away. And so I spend that week wondering why I cannot get away.

For days I perform the magic trick unique to my species. My head and my body are in two different places.

Like some computer-generated animation, my body is on an island where the most important news is the weather report. My head is on the mainland of issues, ideas, policies. My body is dressed in shorts, T-shirt, baseball cap. My mind is in a suit, pantyhose, heels.

I am split across the great divide between this place and the other. Neither here nor there. The desk chair is full, the hammock empty. My focus remains elsewhere.

I fell like a creature of the modern world who has learned to live much—too much—of the time of fast-forward and to pretend that it is a natural rhythm.

What would Charlie Chaplin make of these Modern Times? Our impatience when the computer or the ATM machine "slows" down, or when the plane is late? The way many of us have to do two things at once, to ratchet up our productivity, that buzzword of the era, as if life were an assembly line?

In some recess of this modern times mind-set, I thought I could be on vacation and at work. Instead these two masters wrangle for custody over me and I learned that there are two things you cannot do at once: something and nothing.

But finally, this morning, walking down the country road at a distracted, aerobic, urban speed, I brake for butterflies.

I am aware suddenly of four monarch butterflies in full orange and black

robes at their regal work. They have claimed a weedy plot of milkweeds as their territory.

As I stand absolutely still, these four become 8 and then 12. My eye slowly adjusts to monarchs the way it adjusts to the dark or the way you gradually see blueberries on a green bush.

There are 20 butterflies harvesting a plot no bigger than my desk. Here are 30 in a space smaller than my office. The flock, the herd, has followed its summer taste buds onto my island the way native tribes one came here for the clams. They leave as suddenly as summer people.

I am permitted to watch from inched away. For half a minute, one monarch butterfly chooses my baseball cap as his throne. For half an hour I am not an intruder but part of the native landscape.

Such moments are rare in our world of rapid eye moments. We have been taught to hurry, to scan instead of read, to surf instead of watch.

We can go from zero to 100 miles an hour in seconds—but only by leaving the natural world in the dust.

We pride ourselves on speed—and forget that time goes by fast enough. The trick is to slow down long enough to listen, smell, touch, look, live.

At long last, the faxes and phones and ties all disconnect. And for a summer afternoon, surrounded by monarch butterflies, I know this: I have nothing better to do than watch.

Notes

attachments：依恋
animation：动画
intruder：入侵者

透视 PERCEPTION

停车赏蝶

缅因州的卡斯考海湾——我一路狂飙赶到这里。我平时恨不能将一秒钟都拆开来过,这样的想法终日萦绕于我的脑海,就像是戴上了手表的手腕一样,甩都甩不开。

我身后是一个让人九死一生才能够完成的时间表。飞机晚点了。油箱里没油了。没赶上船。

伴随着工作而来的精神包袱仍然挥之不去,随我一同来岛上度假。我的箱子里装的都是工作,传真机、装有调制解调器的笔记本电脑。我与电脑这个了不起的信息工具难分难舍,它通过电子"食道"给我带来信息快餐。

我便这样全副武装起来,我对自己说我可能得再多休息一个星期。这样我可以利用这段时间想想自己为什么不能抛开与工作有关的一切而尽情享受休闲的时光。

接连几天我都在表演只有我这一类人才熟稔的魔术——"三头六臂之身首异处大魔法"。

我就跟电脑合成的动画似的,身体游荡在小岛上,这里最重要的新闻就是天气预报了。而我的脑袋却还在大陆上转悠,思考着各种各样的问题、见解和政策。我的身体裹在短裤、T恤衫和棒球帽之下,而脑子则装在职业套装、连裤袜和高跟鞋里。

海岛和大陆将我一分为二。我既不在这里也不在那里。我神游到大陆,一屁股"坐"上了办公椅,而海边小吊床却了无"人气"可言。我的关注点仍然在这个小岛之外。

我感觉自己是现代世界的产物，总在学习如何从生活中获取——获取更多，不停地快进以争取更多的时间，并假装这就是生活最自然的韵律。

查理·卓别林会如何演绎这样的"摩登时代"呢？是反映我们当自动取款机速度缓慢时或者飞机晚点时的无奈吗？有很多人习惯了"一心二用"，以此来提高"生产效率"——我们这个时代的热词——俨然将生活变成了生产线。

沉浸在这种现代思维中，我觉得自己可以一边度假一边工作。然而，我着实分心乏术。我终于弄明白了，有两种状态是不可能并存的——忙碌与悠闲。

今天早晨，我走在乡间的小路上，步履烦乱而匆忙，仍旧保持城市的节奏。但是，我却为几只蝴蝶"踩了刹车"。

我突然发现四只穿着橙黄和乌黑长袍的黑脉金斑蝶在工作，很有帝王气派。它们把一块杂草丛生的乳草丛当成了自己的领地。

我就站在那里纹丝不动地欣赏它们，一会儿四只变成了八只，又变成了十二只。我的眼睛慢慢适应了它们，就像适应黑暗或者逐渐看清绿色灌木丛中的蓝莓一样。

那里有二十只蝴蝶，它们辛勤"耕耘"着跟我的办公桌差不多大的地盘。这里还有三十只，它们活动的空间还不及我的办公室大。这一群，那一群，它们跟随着夏天的味蕾来到我度假的这个小岛上，一如当初到这里捕捞蛤蜊的印第安人。它们再和夏天到这里度假的人一起突然离去。

这些蝴蝶允许我在它们咫尺之遥的地方观看它们。一只黑脉金斑蝶把我的棒球帽当成了它的皇帝宝座，在上面足足停留了半分钟。在这半个小时中，我不是一个外来的入侵者，而是自然风景的一部分。

这样的时刻在我们那个瞬息万变的世界里是多么少有的啊。我们早就学会行色匆匆，学会浏览而不是阅读，学会"冲浪"而不是观看。

我们在几秒钟内就可以将车速从零加速到一百迈——却将大自然抛到了九霄云外。

我们以速度快为荣——忘了时间本已过得很快。我们现在所迫切需要的是放慢速度来倾听、嗅闻、触摸、观看和生活。

透视 PERCEPTION

终于,传真、电话以及一切与外界的联络都中断了。在这样一个夏日的午后,我被这些黑脉金斑蝶所包围,我明白了一点:没有比旁观更好的事情了。

More to Read

现实生活中我们有多少人过着古德曼所描绘的忙碌生活——"恨不能将一秒钟都拆开来过",为了提高效率而不停"一心二用"。我们的压力越来越大,时间越来越少;工作越来越忙,快乐越来越少。且看汉字"忙",其左是"心",右是"亡",说的不就是忙、忙、忙,忙到心都死了吗!为了让心不死,不如像古德曼一样放下手中各种未竟之事,给自己忙乱的生活放个假。当我们不以功利来计算生活时,真性情才会得到释放,快乐才会悄然而至。生活中其实有太多"美丽的蝴蝶"值得我们驻足,静静观赏。

Reading Guidance

　　本文作者艾丽丝·沃克是20世纪70年代以来美国文坛最著名的黑人女作家之一。她最有影响力的作品是长篇小说《紫色》(*The Color Purple*),这部作品于1982年发表以后,便引起轰动,并获得了普利策奖、美国国家图书奖和美国全国书评家协会奖三项殊荣。艾丽丝·沃克也由此成为获得普利策奖和美国国家图书奖的第一位黑人女作家。艾丽丝·沃克出生在美国南方佐治亚州的一个佃农家庭。一次,在和哥哥们玩"牛仔与印第安人"的游戏时,她被哥哥的玩具枪射瞎了右眼。当时的她只有8岁。童年的不幸让她的人生从此蒙上了阴影,一个本该天真活泼的小姑娘突然间变得敏感和自卑。直到有一天,3岁女儿的一个发问竟让艾丽丝如释重负,并邂逅了那个久违的美丽的自己。

Beauty: When the Other Dancer Is the Self

　　It is now thirty years since the "accident". A beautiful journalist comes to visit and to interview me. She is going to write a cover story for her magazine that focuses on my latest book. "Decide how you want to look on the cover," she says. "Glamorous, or whatever."

透视 PERCEPTION

Never mind "glamorous", it is the "whatever" that I hear. Suddenly all I can think of is whether I will get enough sleep the night before the photography session: If I don't, my eye will be tired and wander, as blind eyes will.

At night in bed with my lover I think up reasons why I should not appear on the cover of a magazine. "My meanest critics will say I've sold out," I say. "My family will now realize I write scandalous books."

"But what's the real reason you don't want to do this?" he asks.

"Because in all probability," I say in a rush, "my eye won't be straight."

"It will be straight enough," he says. Then, "Besides, I thought you'd made your peace with that."

And I suddenly remember that I have.

I remember:

I am talking to my brother Jimmy, asking if he remembers anything unusual about the day I was shot. "Well," he says, "all I remember is standing by the side of the highway with Daddy, trying to flag down a car. A white man stopped, but when Daddy said he needed somebody to take his little girl to the doctor, he drove off."

I remember:

I am in the desert for the first time. I fall totally in love with it. I am so overwhelmed by its beauty, I confront for the first time, consciously, the meaning of the doctor's words years ago: "Eyes are sympathetic. If one is blind, the other will likely become blind too." I realize I have dashed about the world madly, looking at this, looking at that, storing up images against the fading of the light. But I might have missed seeing the desert! The shock of that possibility—and gratitude for over twenty five years of sight—sends me literally to my knees. Poem after poem comes—which is perhaps how poets pray.

ON SIGHT

I am so thankful I have seen

    The desert
    And the creatures in the desert
    And the desert itself.

    The desert has its own moon
    Which I have seen
    With my own eye.
    There is no flag on it.

    Trees of the desert have arms
    All of which are always up
    That is because the moon is up
    The sun is up also the sky
    The stars clouds none with flags.

    If there were flags,
    I doubt the trees would point.
    Would you?

    But mostly, I remember this:

    I am twenty-seven, and my baby daughter is almost three. Since the birth I have worried about her discovery that her mother's eyes are different from other people's. Will she be embarrassed? I think. What will she say? Every day she watches a television program called *Big Blue Marble*. It begins with a picture of the earth as it appears from the moon. It is bluish, a little battered-looking, but full of light, with whitish clouds swirling around it. Every time I see it I weep with love, as if it is a picture of Grandma's house. One day when I am putting Rebecca down for her nap, she suddenly focuses on my eye. Something inside me cringes, gets ready to try to protect myself. All children are cruel about physical differences, I know from experience, and that they don't always mean to be is another matter. I assume Rebecca will be the same.

But no-o-o-o. She studies my face intently as we stand, her inside and me outside her crib. She even holds my face maternally between her dimpled little hands. Then, looking every bit as serious and lawyerlike as her father, she says, as if it may just possibly have slipped my attention: "Mommy, there's a world in your eye." (As in, "Don't be alarmed, or do anything crazy.") And then, gently, but with great interest: "Mommy, where did you get that world in your eye?"

For the most part, the pain left then. Crying and laughing I ran to the bathroom, while Rebecca mumbled and sang herself to sleep. Yes indeed, I realized, looking into the mirror. There was a world in my eye. And I saw that it was possible to love it.

That night I dream I am dancing. As I dance, whirling and joyous, happier than I've ever been in my life, another bright-faced dancer joins me. We dance and kiss each other and hold each other through the night. The other dancer has obviously come through all right, as I have done. She is beautiful, whole, and free. And she is also me.

Notes

bluish:接近蓝色的,浅蓝的
cringe:畏缩,退缩
maternally:母亲般地

美：当另一位舞者是自己

　　这场"意外"已经过去 30 年了。一位漂亮的记者来采访我。她要在杂志中写一篇跟我的新书有关的封面故事。"你看你的封面照片想拍成什么样子？"她问道："迷人或是别的什么。"

　　"迷人"还是别想了，我听见的只有"别的什么"。我突然想到的是在拍封面照片的前夜，自己是否能睡个安稳觉。要是睡眠不足，我的那只眼睛就会显得疲惫而游移，看上去就真跟瞎了似的。

　　晚上，我跟爱人躺在床上，细数我无论如何不能登上封面的种种理由。"那些不看好我的评论家会说我认输了。""我的家人会以为我在写些乌七八糟的书呢。"

　　"可真正的原因又是什么呢？"他问。

　　我急忙说："我的眼睛有问题。"

　　"你的眼睛根本没问题，"他说："我本以为你已经彻底释然了呢。"

　　这时，我突然想起好像是这样的。

　　是的，我想起来了。

　　我跟弟弟吉米聊天，问他是否还记得我的眼睛被子弹射中的那天有什么异样？他说："我只记得和爸爸站在路边，拦车来着。一个白人男子停下了车，不过当爸爸说想让他帮忙把女儿送到医院时，他一溜烟开走了。"

　　我记得：

　　我生平第一次去沙漠，我彻底爱上了它，它的美令我折服。我第一次真正理解了医生几年前对我说的话："双眼是惺惺相惜的。其中一只失明了，另一只也有可能失明。"我满世界狂奔，一会儿看看这，一会儿看看那，

透视 PERCEPTION

在视力模糊前，我要把看到的一切都存储在记忆之中。或许，我以后就再也看不见沙漠了！这种可能性所带给我的震动以及对 25 年来我所感知到的光明的感激之情让我着实跪倒在地去祈祷。这时我诗兴大发——诗人大概都是这么祈祷的。

光明
我感激自己能够看到
沙漠，
沙漠中的生灵，
和这茫茫沙漠。

沙漠有自己的月亮，
我看见了，
用我自己的眼睛，
没有翳障。

沙漠的树木都有手臂，
向上伸展着。
因为月亮在它们头顶，
太阳也在头顶，
还有整个天空，
星星，
云彩，
全都没有翳障。

即便有翳障，我怀疑，
树木们仍然会向上伸展，
是不是？

但是，我最记得的是：

我 27 岁那年，我的宝贝女儿瑞贝卡快 3 岁了。自女儿出生以来，我就担心她发现自己妈妈的眼睛与众不同。她会觉得很尴尬吗？我想。她会怎么说呢？每天她都会收看一档名为《巨大蓝色弹珠》的儿童电视节目。片头是一幅在月球上拍到的地球图像，它是蓝绿色的，看上去有点扭曲，但是却很光亮，而且有云雾缭绕。每次我看到它，都因感到同病相怜而禁不住哭泣，就像看见那张祖母房子的老照片一样。有一天，我把昏昏欲睡的瑞贝卡放下时，她突然凝视着我的那只眼睛。我的内心一阵刺痛，想着怎么向她解释。从我的经验来看，小孩对生理上的与众不同是很刻薄的，尽管他们是无心的。我猜想瑞贝卡大概也是这样的。

但，不是，不是我想的那样。我站在那里，她关切地打量着我的脸。她在小摇篮里，我在小摇篮外。她那满是窝窝的小胖手甚至还充满母性，温柔地捧起我的脸庞。她特认真，生怕我会心不在焉，这有些像她的律师爸爸，她对我说："妈妈，你的眼睛里有一个世界。"（语气就像在说"别慌，或者别做傻事"。）接着，她又饶有兴致地问："妈妈，你眼睛里的那个世界是从哪里来的呀？"

就这一句话让我所有的痛苦都烟消云散了。我跑到卫生间又哭又笑，这时瑞贝卡咿咿呀呀地把自己给唱睡着了。我看着镜子中的自己，就是啊，我的眼睛里有一个世界。我明白了我是有可能爱上这只眼睛的。

那晚，我梦见自己翩翩起舞。我旋转着，快乐地舞着，比我一生中其他时候都快乐，这时另一个晶莹剔透的面庞加入进来。我们一起跳舞，互相亲吻，整晚都相拥在一起。那个舞者跟我步调一致。她美丽，健康，而且自由——她就是我。

透视 PERCEPTION

More to Read

　　幸福的人生每每相似，不幸的人生各有不同。艾丽丝·沃克的不幸起源于童年的那场飞来横祸。或许，对于她来说，人生最可怕的不是黑暗，而是对光明的祭奠。那些失明以前的记忆永远刻在心间，每想起一次就会痛彻心扉。然而，沃克最终找到了她的光明，她可以和不完美的自己握手言和，相拥起舞。而这一切全都归功于她3岁的女儿，女儿用她的天真无邪拨开了压在母亲心头多年的阴翳，让温暖的阳光照进了现实。

Reading Guidance

本文作者狄波拉·奥莉薇亚是美国记者,在法国生活了十多年,嫁给了一个法国人,育有两子。现奔走于洛杉矶和巴黎两地,大部分时间都在反思美国和法国女人之间的差异。为什么大家都说法国女人有魅力,让人目眩神迷?为什么她们那么时髦可爱、窈窕动人?在此,作者为我们一一解码。为了更好地理解文章内容,读者有必要了解一些相关背景知识。玛丽·安托瓦尼特(Marie Antoinette)是法国国王路易十六的王后,她一直是奢侈、放纵的代名词,根据历史记载,这位王后因挥霍无度而使国家债台高筑,最后被革命者送上了断头台。雪维安·爱嘉辛斯基(Sylviane Agacinski)是法国哲学家、女权主义者,也是法国高等社会科学院的教授,她的丈夫是法国前总理贝尔纳·库什内。

Unlocking the Secrets of French Women

Even before Marie Antoinette's head ended up in a basket, we've been intrigued by French women. Witness the waves of books about them that continue to be written. But why, truly, do these creatures have such enduring cachet in the hall of fame of sexiness and allure? There are many myths and clichés about them that simply aren't true, after all. French women do get fat. They're not all femme fatales. They don't invest half their life savings in lingerie.

Then again, there is something about French women we just can't seem to define. It's called, famously and appropriately enough, that "je ne sais quoi"— or, literally translated, that "I don't know what". After living more than a decade among the Gauls, I was more interested in the culturally-brewed realities behind that infuriating term. Here are a few byte-size samples.

French women are self-possessed; even slightly defiant. Why? Partly because they don't grow up with the mandate to be liked and be like everyone else. There's no word or concept for "popularity" in France. Imagine growing up without that pressure. No wonder French women don't seem to give a damn what we think of them. When it comes to relationships, that self-possession serves them well.

Where we grow up picking flowers and pondering love with "He loves me, he loves me not," the French grow up with this refrain: "He love me a little. A lot. Passionately. Madly. Not at all." How unfair. We think in terms of total love or absolute rejection. They think in degrees of passion and possibility.

French feminist Sylviane Agacinski once said: "We want the power to seduce and be seduced. There will never be a war of the sexes in France." (Likewise, Louis XIV of France once declared: "Under a king, a country is really ruled by a woman.") And so it is. French men and women actually like each other. A lot. Flirtation is a civic duty in France, not a menace. French women generally prefer men to be in the picture, not out of it.

The pursuit of happiness is written into our constitution and the happy ending is written into our culture. Not so in France. The French are suspicious of happily-ever-after and exalted standards of happiness or moral perfection. They're simultaneously romantic and realistic. If something seems too good to be true, the French tend to think that it's not.

The French enjoy being grown-ups. They do not believe in being forever

young. You will never see a French woman wearing a T-shirt that says "Life begins at seventy".

French women are matter-of-fact about the body. Contrary to popular opinion, they do not dramatize or sensationalize sex. They're also not any more adulterous than we are; they're simply more willing to concede that passion grows in unexpected places. ("The French are marathoners, and Americans are sprinters," according to one researcher. In other words, we all push the marital envelope; we just wear different running shoes.)

The French don't covet packaged cookie-cutter beauty, au naturel is de rigeur, and less is truly more in France.

These are, of course, the more redeeming aspects of French women. There are many reasons to love and hate the French, and countless books have been written about the latter part of that sentence. The point here is not to exalt French (though they do have a peculiar tendency to provoke extreme reactions in us), but to consider what we might learn from their cultural attributes—because as Descartes once put it, it is "good to know something of the customs of different people in order to judge more soundly of our own."

Notes

cachet：威信，声望
lingerie：女子贴身内衣或睡衣
self-possession：沉着

透视 PERCEPTION

掀开她们的面纱

人们对于法国女人的兴趣早在玛丽王后被送上断头台前就开始了。关于法国女人的书此消彼长,一浪高过一浪。为什么这些尤物能够一直是性感、魅力的代言人呢?当然,很多关于她们的说法并不可信。法国女人也是会发胖的。她们也不都是"害人精",她们也并不一定会将自己的半生积蓄都用来购买内衣。

关于法国女人,有些事还真不好去定义,最确切也最流行的说法就是"我也不知道是什么"。在高卢人周围生活了十多年后,我对那些由文化因素所催生的现实的兴趣更为浓厚,这些都能很好地解释"我也不知道是什么"这一说法。在此,仅举几例。

法国女人沉着冷静,甚至有些反叛。为什么会这样?大概是因为在她们成长的过程中,并不刻意地迎合别人,或者期望博得所有人的喜爱。在法语中没有"受欢迎"一词或概念。想想在没有这种压力下成长会是什么样子吧。难怪法国女人根本不在意我们如何看她们。在人际关系中,法国女人的冷静让她们受益匪浅。

当我们一边摘花,一边暗自思忖"他爱我,他不爱我"这样的问题时,法国女人对爱情表现得很是克制,用词也很精准:"他有点喜欢我。他很喜欢我。他对我很有兴趣。他疯狂地爱上我。他一点也不喜欢我。"太不公平了。我们所想的要么是一心一意地爱,要么是毅然决然地回绝。但是,法国女人所思考的是感情的可能性和浓度。

法国的女权主义者雪维安·爱嘉辛斯基曾说:"我们想拥有让人着迷的能力,也需要为别人着迷。在法国永远都不会有两性大战。"(与之相似,法国的国王路易十四曾经宣称:"国王虽为一国之君,但是一个国家真正的统治者是女人。")的确如此。法国男人和女人确实互相倾慕。在法国,打情骂俏是公民义务,并不令人反感。法国女人大都希望男人出现在她们的生活画卷中,而不是拒他们于千里之外。

追求幸福被写进我们的宪法,而童话般完美的结局也深深植根于我们的文化。法国却并不是这样。法国女人怀疑完美的结局,也不相信崇高的幸福标准或者完美的道德准则。她们既浪漫又现实。如果有些事情太过美好而显得不真实,那么法国女人宁信其无,而不信其有。

法国女人享受成长,而不卖"萌"。她们不相信长生不老。你永远也不会看到法国女人穿着印有"70岁,人生才刚刚起步"这样语句的T恤衫。

法国女人对于身体是很认真的。与人们普遍的想法不同的是,法国女人不喜欢夸大和渲染男欢女爱。她们并不是传说中的那么不忠贞,她们只不过更愿意承认自己在意想不到的地方萌生了爱意。(一个研究人员说:"法国人擅长马拉松,而美国人对短跑更拿手。"换言之,无论法国人还是美国人,都会打开婚姻这个信封,只是穿着不同的跑鞋而已。)

法国女人并不希求绝世的美貌,在法国,自然就是美,少即是多。

当然,这些都是在为法国女人开脱。我们有太多的理由去爱抑或是恨法国女人。也有很多书是关于这句话后半句的(即恨法国女人)。我在这里并不想为法国女人唱赞歌(尽管她们很容易让我们有极端的反应),而是要仔细思考一下我们应该从她们的文化特色中学到些什么——正如笛卡尔所说:"了解其他民族的习惯和传统是为了更好地认知自己。"

More to Read

  本文作者从具体的事例展开对于法国女性的评述,其间也将她们和美国女性进行了对比。她的言语之间流露出自然、平和,又不乏幽默的味道,使读者在阅读时一会儿点头称是,一会儿莞尔一笑。透过文字,我们可以感受到法国文化的特质,尤其是法国女人的魅力,这不仅感染了作者,更浸润了她的个性和笔触。因为,对于观察对象的一种好奇和认同在大多数情况下都意味着观察者在行为上的一种改进,孔子所说的"见贤思齐"就是这个道理。不仅如此,作者在文末所引用的笛卡尔的名言也为她的文化观察与比较提供了更为高远的立意。是的,比较只是手段而不是目的。法国女人好像一面镜子,透过她们,我们所看到的应该是自己,我们所应该做的是深刻的自省。

Reading Guidance

　　本文的作者很有幽默感,而且幽默之中带着些许辛辣的讽刺。在某些地方,作者的想法会让人忍俊不禁。文中出现了很多文化名词,可能会给读者造成一定困难。现做一一解释。"Pinkstinks"是一项社会运动,以挑战入侵女孩子生活的"粉色文化"为目标,致力于为女孩子寻找真正值得学习的偶像,让她们在生活中拥有更为严肃的追求,更为关注自身能力的提升,而不只是站在镜子前顾影自怜。"Early Learning Center"是英国的儿童玩具连锁店,所出售的玩具兼具游戏、教育和开发功能。"WAG"是"wives and girlfriends"的首字母缩写,是英国小报对职业足球运动员的老婆或女友的称呼,最初专指英国球员的家属。该词汇首次被大量使用是在2006年的世界杯上。"Morticia Addams"是漫画家查尔斯·亚当斯在漫画《亚当斯一家》中所虚构的形象,一袭黑衣是她的招牌装扮。"Morticia"这个名字寓意"死亡"。"Toys 'R' Us"是美国的儿童玩具连锁店,总部在新泽西州的韦恩市。其中"R"是英文"are"的缩写。

Why Pink Doesn't Stink

　　The commoditisation of pink shouldn't taint our feelings towards indulging girls' taste for it. After all, it didn't stop Barbara Cartland.

Pink is on the brink. According to a new campaign group called Pinkstinks, "the culture of pink invades every aspect of girls' lives", and the relentless march of pinkification must be stopped before the nation's six-year-olds set out, en masse, to shred the last 50 years of the women's movement by setting their hearts on careers as manicurists and go-go dancers in a rose-tinted haze of glee for girliness.

Justice minister Bridget Prentice has pledged her support to the campaign. "It's about not funnelling girls into pretty, pretty jobs, but about giving them aspirations and challenging them to fulfil their potential," she said. "We want to say to organizations like the Early Learning Centre that we rely on them to be progressive about encouraging girls to think of themselves as equal, and not to reinforce the old stereotypes."

This is all well and good, but what's the colour got to do with it? When I was a child, I loved pink. Couldn't get enough of it. Granma would dress me in pink frilly knickers. Mum would get me home and change them immediately. At seven, I was demented in desire for a pink Barbie bath set. My mother, a staunch feminist, screamed with her face pressed into a cushion when aunty Sara bought me one for what seemed at the time my best birthday ever.

But I'm over it. Nowadays I'm working as a journalist—as opposed to queuing up outside Boujis every night on a great, glittering quest to become a WAG—and go to work dressed head to toe in black (appropriate attire for working in an industry so perky right now that one may as well be working in an undertaker's and taking style tips from Morticia Adams).

For some reason little girls really like pink. They like princesses and ponies and perfume and pastel and all sorts of other horrible things that make adult feminists wince. But they grow out of it. No one appears to be suggesting that boys will grow up wanting to be wrestlers due to the noxious influence of the WWE figures on offer for them at Toys "R" Us.

Yet Emma Moore, co-founder of Pinkstinks, is adamant. "Ask yourself

what we want girls and boys to learn from an early age. Is it that pink, passive and pretty is for girls and that blue, bold and challenging is for boys?" Interestingly, until the 1940s pink was apparently used to dress boys as blue was seen as a more dainty and delicate colour appropriate for girls.

But pink itself is no bad thing: Picasso had a pink period; Pink Floyd were a great band; gay pride has adopted pink as its colour; in Thailand it is, apparently, the colour of those born on a Tuesday; Elvis drove a pink Cadillac.

The late high priestess of pink, the chiffon dame, Barbara Cartland—who uniquely favoured the colour following a trip to Tutankamen's tomb in the 1920s, where she liked the tint of the walls so much that she forsook all other colours—didn't let the dainty shade curb her ambition. On average she wrote a novel a fortnight, and appears in *The Guinness Book of Records* as the world's most prolific novelist, with estimated worldwide sales of one billion copies in 36 languages. As Christian Dior once noted: "Pink will prevail."

Notes

relentless: 不停的, 持续的

shred: 撕裂

stereotype: 陈词滥调

dainty: 精致的, 娇俏的

透视 PERCEPTION

粉色可不恶心

商业化后的粉色不应该玷污我们对迷恋粉色的小女孩的品位的评判。至少,这不会让芭芭拉·卡特兰德停止对粉色的钟爱。

粉色现在正处于风口浪尖。一个刚刚成立的组织"恶心的粉色"是这样蛊惑人心的:"粉色文化侵蚀了女孩子生活的方方面面,无孔不入。"在我们国家的 6 岁女童开始大规模断送过去 50 年妇女解放运动的硕果之前,在她们为追求所谓的女孩味道而热衷于美甲师、摇摆舞演员这些职业之前,粉色化大踏步的进程必须被及时阻止。

司法部长布丽奇特·普伦蒂斯承诺将大力支持这场运动。"这并不是说要让大批的女孩子出去工作,而是要给她们更为高远的志向,激发她们去发掘自己内心的潜力。"她说:"我们想要对类似早期学习中心这样的机构说,我们要仰仗它们不断地鼓励女孩子们把自己当做与男人平起平坐的独立个体来看待,而不要为过去那些陈词滥调推波助澜。"

这么做当然很好。然而,颜色跟这些有何关系?我小时候就喜爱粉色,而且绝对属于爱不释手、不能自拔那种。我的奶奶会给我穿粉色镶边的灯笼裤。而妈妈却会把我领回家,立刻将我的粉裤子换下。7 岁时,我疯狂迷上了芭比的粉色浴室组合玩具。后来,莎拉阿姨在我生日时送了我一套,当时真的没有比这更对我心思的礼物了。可是,我那位不折不扣的女权主义的妈妈看到后的第一反应是把脸埋在沙发靠垫里尖叫不已。

现在一切都已成往事。我当了记者,整天从头到脚一袭黑衣外出工作(现在这种打扮在职场很流行,看着就像是干殡仪业的,要么就是得了梦迪西亚·亚当斯的着装真传,跟个死人似的)。我也不会站在伦敦布吉斯夜总会的门口排队,梦想着成为某个足球运动员的女友或妻子。

　　出于某种原因,女孩子确实是很喜欢粉色。她们喜欢公主、小马驹、香水、彩色蜡笔和所有让成年女权主义者惟恐避之不及的东西。但是,她们就是在这些东西的包围中成长起来的。怎么没有人说男孩子会受到玩具城出售的美国职业摔跤人偶的毒害转而想要成为摔跤手呢?

　　"恶心的粉色"这一组织的创办人艾玛·摩尔是铁了心地讨厌粉色。她说:"问问你们自己希望孩子在小时候学些什么吧。我们是不是告诉他们粉色、被动、漂亮代表女孩子;蓝色、勇敢、接受挑战代表男孩子?"然而,有趣的是,直到20世纪40年代,粉色还被用在男孩子的服装上,因为人们认为蓝色更为雅致、娇俏,更适合女孩子。

　　粉色本身并没有错:毕加索曾经有过粉色情结;粉色的弗洛伊德是个了不起的乐队;同性恋者也把粉色视为自己身份的象征;在泰国,粉色是那些周二出生的人的幸运色;猫王以前开的是辆粉色的凯迪拉克……

　　已故"粉色教主"、"雪纺夫人"芭芭拉·卡特兰德对粉色更是情有独钟。20世纪20年代,她曾经到埃及法老图坦卡蒙的金字塔一游,她很喜欢墓室墙壁淡淡的粉色,以至于回来后只钟情于粉色,而对其他颜色都弃若敝屣。然而,娇俏的粉色衣衫并没有阻碍她的雄心壮志啊。她平均每两个星期就能写出一部小说。作为世界上最多产的小说家,她还被载入了吉尼斯世界纪录。她的小说被翻译成36种语言,销量有10亿册之多。正如克里斯汀·迪奥曾经所言:"粉色注定流行。"

More to Read

粉色对你来说意味着什么？温柔、浪漫、轻浮抑或是纯真。我喜欢粉色，我甚至还有一双漂亮的粉色鞋子，所不同的是我现在足够成熟，我知道我虽然穿着粉色的鞋子，但我仍能改变世界。在这个充满活力与种种可能性的世界上，不存在男孩的颜色或女孩的颜色，蓝色、粉色仅仅是颜色而已。也没有专属男孩的玩具或专属女孩的玩具，有的只是玩具。何必把什么都贴上标签。有时候这些无聊的标签就像一件紧身的"珍珠衫"，捆绑住了我们的身体，更束缚了我们的视野。

Reading Guidance

本文讲述的是现在可能已经被人们遗忘的游戏——纵横字谜。原来,这方寸之间有这么多鲜为人知的精彩故事。作者在文中详细回顾了纵横字谜的发展历史,同时也为我们道出了很多有趣的出谜准则和宗旨。置身于这小小的字谜中,我们看到了大众文化的一点缩影。同时,也借由作者的描述,体会到了美国人对纵横字谜的喜爱与迷恋。看似简单的游戏对脑力也是一个不小的挑战呢!读读这篇文章,温暖的怀旧情绪会油然而生。你是不是想起了儿时常玩的那些简单、质朴的游戏呢?

Crazy Over Crosswords

Every Day, millions of Americans escape to a flat, rectangular world, where every problem has a solution. This is a world in which the people wear Japanese sashes called obis and live in a Chinese pagoda called a taa. Most of the work is performed by feudal slaves, called esnes, which leaves everyone else a lot of time to worship gods and goddesses like Hera, Odin and Thor…

Where is this nicely ordered world? In the crossword puzzle/quiz/riddle…

Nearly every one of the nation's 1,700 daily newspapers has a crossword puzzle, and there are more than 100 crossword-puzzle magazines. It's estimated that over 30 million Americans do crosswords and that's not counting the faint-of-heart who quickly give up when asked for a four-letter word for a Malayan outrigger (proa). In 1980, when the *Los Angeles Times* replaced its Sunday crossword with a puns-and-anagrams feature, more than 3,000 angry calls and letters poured in. The editors immediately backed down.

The Oxford Guide to Word Games calls the crossword the most popular and widespread word game in the world, and puzzles now exist in almost every language. Last May a person guard in Belgium, Roger Bouckaert, unveiled one of the world's largest crossword puzzles over 50,000 words and more than 100 feet long. He said he spent five hours a day for almost four years putting it together.

The first crossword puzzle was a Christmas gift of sorts. Arthur Wynne, an editor for the *New York World*, was looking for a way to liven up the Christmas edition of the Sunday magazine. He drew a diamond-shaped grid and, before long, had fashioned a puzzle of 32 interlocking words that he called word-cross, which made its world debut on December 21, 1913.

Word-cross became a regular Sunday feature, but the game didn't really take off nationally until 1924, when a new publisher, Simon & Schuster, brought out the first crossword-puzzle book. The public response was overwhelming. The company's small office was flooded with mail orders. By year end, Simon & Schuster had published three crossword-puzzle books with sales of over 400,000.

Crosswords had become a national obsession. Books of puzzles, plus dictionaries and the thesaurus, became standard supplies on steamers crossing the Atlantic. The Pennsylvania Railroad printed crosswords on the back of its dining-car menus. Women wore black-and-white dresses with crossword motifs, gold crossword bracelets sold for $35, and there were also wrist dictionaries worn like watches. There was even a Broadway revue called *Puzzles of 1925* that included a scene in a crossword-puzzle sanitarium for people driven mad by the game.

The mania spread across the Atlantic at about the same time. Soon, exasperated London Zoo officials announced they would no longer answer questions about gnus, emus or any other animals of three letters.

By the 1940s, crosswords in this country had become unimaginative and predictable. Fortunately, a new group of puzzlemakers appeared. Instead of cluing "bee" as "stinging insect", puzzlemaker Jack Luzzatto, for example, used "nectar inspector", and he offered "two pints make one cawort" as the clue for "champagne". Rather than cluing "nest" as "bird's home", another innovator chose "nutcracker's suite".

Ironically, the crossword's revival was led by the last major newspaper in America to hold out against the craze—*The New York Times*, which relented in 1942 and started a Sunday puzzle page. Crossword editor Margaret Farrar helped establish many of the current rules and standards for a good puzzle: all-over interlock, meaning the grid is entirely interconnected; no two-letter words; and the fewer the word entries, the better. She used hidden meanings, puzzle themes, and phrases, proper names and foreign terms.

The *Time* didn't start its daily crossword until 1950, but the newspaper's Sunday and daily puzzles soon established themselves as the American standard for excellence. The position of the *Times*' crossword editor became the most prestigious in all of puzzle kingdom. It has been held by only three people in nearly a half-century: Margaret Farrar, who was succeeded by Will Weng in 1969, and the present editor, Eugene T. Maleska, who succeeded Weng in 1977. Maleska's readers are relentless. When Maleska was awakened by an intern at 6 a.m. to autograph a puzzle!

Crossword editors now usually work with free-lance puzzlemakers, some of whom call themselves cruciverbalists. Puzzlemaking is a hobby. The *Washington Post*'s puzzle contributors, for example, include a piano teacher, building contractor and musician. The *New York Times* gets material from homemakers, a convict, an actor and a judge.

Usually the job of the editor is to revise the clues—for the real art of puzzlemaking is in the definitions. "Boston jetsam" can be "tea"; "roads scholar" can be "hobo"; and "fiddler on the reef" can be "crab".

Editors also turn out their own puzzles. William Lutwiniak, co-editor of the *Washington Post* Sunday Magazine crossword, is considered the most prolific cruciverbalist of all time, with more than 7,600 puzzles to his credit. A former cryptologist with the National Security Agency, Lutwiniak wowed the 1987 *Baltimore Crossword Open Tournament* by creating the words for a 15-square-aross and 15-square-down puzzle in 13 minutes and 9 seconds; it took him another 3 minutes to clue the words.

Puzzle editors abide not only by a body of rules but also by a code of ethics. It is considered very bad form to have two obscure words intersecting. And, as much as possible, the puzzlemaker should avoid words plucked from the darkest corners of the dictionary. Crosswords must continually evolve, but the field is dominated by the knowledge of popular culture.

Notes

feature：特写文章，特辑
obsession：痴迷，着魔，困扰
revue：时事讽刺剧

黑白之恋

　　每天数百万美国人躲在一个矩形平面世界中,在那个世界里,日本人穿的腰带叫做宽腰带,中国宝塔叫做塔,做苦力的封建奴隶叫做奴仆,他们建造令人崇拜的如赫拉、欧丁或雷神等神祇的神庙。

　　这个秩序井然的世界到底是哪里?答案就是纵横字谜。

　　美国有 1700 份日报,几乎每份都有纵横字谜版块,另外还有 100 多份专门的字谜杂志。据测超过 3000 万美国人喜欢纵横字谜,这还不包括那些当被问到一个意思是马来西亚人的舷外支架船的四字单词(快速帆船)时就意志薄弱、很快放弃的人。1980 年,《洛杉矶时报》将纵横字谜专栏换为双关语和片语专栏时,收到了 3000 余份投诉电话和信件。编辑立刻将报纸恢复原状了。

　　《牛津文字游戏指南》称纵横字谜是世界上最流行和传播最广的文字游戏,使用的语言已经覆盖了全球所有语言。去年 5 月,一个比利时保安罗杰·布科尔特做出了世界最大的纵横字谜——包括 5 万多个词,100 英尺长。他说,他每天花 5 个小时,做了 4 年才最终完成。

　　1913 年 12 月 21 日,世界上第一个纵横字谜作为圣诞礼物出现在《纽约世界》的周末增刊上。当时的编辑亚瑟·韦恩希望以此来提高杂志圣诞特刊的销量。他画出一个菱形的格子,再配上 32 个彼此相关联的单词,他管它叫单词链。这就是纵横字谜的处子秀。

　　单词链从此成为周末增刊的固有专栏,但是直到 1924 年它才在全国普及。新出版商西蒙和舒斯特尔出版了第一本纵横字谜书。书的反响好极了。公司办公室堆满了邮购订单。到年底时,该出版社已经出版了三本字谜书，销量超过 40 万册。

不久纵横字谜又成为了国际性的游戏，和字典、百科全书一起跨越大西洋成了外销品。宾夕法尼亚铁路公司将纵横字谜印在餐车菜单的背面。妇女们穿着以纵横字谜为主题的时装，纵横字谜的金手镯售价 35 美元，市面上还出现了一种像手表一样的腕上字典。百老汇甚至还上演了一部叫《谜语 1925》的讽刺剧，其中一幕是以专门治疗玩字谜成瘾病人的疗养院为背景的。

同一时期的大洋彼岸，纵横字谜也同样火热。很快，恼羞成怒的伦敦动物园工作人员就宣布他们再也不回答关于角马（gnu）、鸸鹋（emu）等其他任何名字是三个字母的动物的问题。

19 世纪 40 年代，美国的纵横字谜开始变得枯燥乏味、了无新意。幸好这时出现了一群新的出谜人。比如，"蜜蜂"一词的线索不再是"带刺的昆虫"，出谜人杰克·卢札托使用的是"花蜜巡查员"，他还用"使你喝上两品脱就能欢呼雀跃的东西"形容"香槟"。另一位革新者用"星鸟的套房"而不是"鸟类的家"描绘"鸟巢"一词。

具有讽刺意味的是，使纵横字谜幸存下来并再次引起狂热的是美国出现最晚但又是当今主要报纸之一的发行于 1942 年的《纽约时报》。在周末字谜版，字谜编辑玛格丽特·法勒制定了许多现代纵横字谜的出题规范：单词得有交叉，即格子整体要连着；不用只有两个字母的单词；尽量不用单词的复数形式。她使用了单词的引申义、谜语主题、词组、固有名称和外语。

1950 年，日常版的《时代》也有了纵横字谜版块。但是周日版的纵横字谜把自己定位为全国字谜的模范。《时代》杂志字谜编辑成为谜语界声望最高的人。半个世纪以来只有三个人担任过此职务：玛格丽特·法勒；她的继任，1969 年上任的威尔·翁及 1977 年上任的现任编辑尤金·T. 梅尔斯嘉。梅尔斯嘉常常在早晨 6 点就被实习生叫起来在即将刊出的字谜上签字，每当这个时候他就觉得他的读者简直无情透了。

现在的编辑们常常使用自由撰稿人送来的谜语，他们中的一些人管自己叫咬文嚼字出谜人。编谜语是一种爱好。比如，为《华盛顿邮报》贡献字谜的人包括钢琴教师、建筑承包商和音乐人。《纽约时报》则从家庭主妇、罪犯、演员和法官那里得到谜语。

编辑通常只是整理暗示，因为真正意义上的编谜语就是指编出那些暗示。"波士顿漂流物"是"茶"，"公路学者"是"流浪汉"，"暗礁上的拉琴人"指的就是"螃蟹"。

编辑自己也编字谜。《华盛顿邮报》周末特刊纵横字谜联合编辑威廉·路德维尼亚克是公认的最高产的咬文嚼字出谜人，他创造过7600个字谜。作为前国家安全顾问的密友，路德维尼亚克曾在13分9秒里创造了一个15米宽15米长的字谜，又用了3分钟给出提示，此举给1987年巴尔的摩纵横字谜公开赛添上了华美的一笔。

除了一套出题规则，字谜编辑还有一套道德规范需要遵守。比如把两个朦胧的词联系在一起是很不好的。出谜者也应该尽量避免使用那些极为生僻的词汇。纵横字谜应该得到不断发展，但是涉及的内容应该是大众熟悉的知识。

More to Read

闲来无事时，我们中国人似乎更喜欢来自日本的"卡拉OK"，三五好友一起高唱至天明很是快意；要不就是挂在网上，大玩网络游戏，很"宅"。像文章所说的痴迷于字谜游戏的人实在是屈指可数，真要是看见有人在玩字谜，我们恐怕会怀疑自己是不是穿越到了古代——有没有搞错。是的，在信息科技时代，我们的娱乐方式瞬息万变，令人眼花缭乱。刚放下《反恐精英》，又出来了《愤怒的小鸟》。"不是我不明白，这世界变化快。"纵横字谜游戏跟这些高科技产物相比真是太土了。不过，也正因为如此，这篇文章才会给人以耳目一新的亲切感觉，让我们能够暂且突出科技的重围，重温这种纯粹的思考带给我们的快感。

透 视 PERCEPTION

Reading Guidance

"SUV"是英文"Sport Utility Vehicle"的首字母缩写,指的是运动型多功能汽车。"SUV"起源于美国,同样也是近年美国市场最畅销的车型。20 世纪 80 年代,"SUV"是为迎合年轻白领阶层的爱好,在皮卡(pickup)底盘上发展起来的一种厢式车。"SUV"采用四轮驱动,一般前悬挂是轿车车型的独立螺旋弹簧悬架;后悬挂则是非独立钢板弹簧悬架,离地间隙较大;在一定程度上既有轿车的舒适性,又有越野车的越野性能。这类车既可载人,又可载货,行驶范围广,具有豪华轿车的功能。文中,作者从汽车广告入手,为读者描绘了一幅关于汽车文化的超现实主义画卷。广告中的生活是令人心驰神往的,在这种美好的气氛中,无奈的现实渐渐走进视野。作者所使用的是典型的先扬后抑、欲擒故纵的写作手法,以此来引发读者对运动型多功能汽车日渐流行这一城市文化现象的思考。

SUVs: Killer Cars

For my second career, I want to write car ads. Or better yet, I want to live in a car ad.

In the real world, you and I creep and beep on some misnomered expressway, but in the commercial fantasy land, drivers cruise along deserted, tree-

lined roads.

We stall and crawl on city streets, but the man in the Lexus races "in the fast lane"—on an elevated road that curves around skyscrapers. We circle the block, looking for a place to park, but the owner of a Toyota RAV4 pulls up onto the sandy beach, we get stuck in the tunnel, but the Escalade man navigates down empty streets because "there are no roadblocks".

The world of the car ads bears about as much resemblance to commuter life as the Marlboro ads bear to the cancer ward.

All of this is a prelude to a full-boil rant against the archenemy of commuters everywhere: sport utility vehicles. Yes, those gas-guzzling, parking space-hogging, bullies of the highway.

These sport utility vehicles are bought primarily by people whose favorite sport is shopping and whose most rugged athletic event is hauling the kids to soccer practice.

The sales and the size of the larger SUVs have grown at a speed that reminds me of the defense budget. In the escalating highway arms race, SUVs are sold for self-defense. Against what? Other SUVs.

As someone who has spent many a traffic-jammed day in the shadow of a behemoth, I am not surprised that the high and weighty are responsible for some 2,000 additional deaths a year. If a 6,000-pound Suburban hits a 1,800-pound Metro, it's going to be bad for the Metro. For that matter, if the Metro hits the Suburban, it's still going to be bad for the Metro.

The problem with SUVs is that you can't see over them, you can't see around them and you have to watch out for them. I am by no means the only driver of a small car who has felt intimidated by the big wheels barreling past me. Their macho reputation prompted even the Automobile Club of Southern California to issue an SUV drivers tip: "Avoid a 'road warrior' mentality. Some SUV drivers operate under the false illusion that they can ignore common rules of caution."

透视 PERCEPTION

But the biggest and burliest of the pack aren't safety hazards; they're environmental hazards. Until now, SUVs have been allowed to legally pollute two or three times as much as automobiles. All over suburbia there are people who conscientiously drive their empty bottles to the suburban recycling center in vehicles that get 15 miles to the gallon. There are parents putting big bucks down for a big car so the kids can be safe while the air they breathe is being polluted.

At long last some small controls are being promoted. The EPA has proposed for the first time that SUVs be treated like urban won't be allowed to emit more than a Taurus. That's an important beginning, but not the whole story.

Consider Ford, for example. The automaker produces relatively clean-burning engines. But this fall it will introduce the humongous Excursion. It's 7 feet tall, 80 inches wide, weights 4 tons and gets 10 miles to the gallon in the city. No wonder the Sierra Club calls it "the Ford Valdez". This is a nice car for taking the kids to school—if you're afraid you'll run into a tank.

I wouldn't go that far, though I have wished that hot trip on at least one SUV whose bumper came to eye level with my windshield. Still, the SUV backlash is growing so strong that today's status symbol may become the first socially unacceptable vehicle since cars lost their fins.

It's one thing to have an SUV in the outback and quite another to drive it around town. In the end, the right place for the big guy is in the car ad. There, the skies are always clean, the drivers are always relaxed and there's never, ever another car in sight.

Notes

misnomer:使用不当,用词错误
resemblance:相似,形似
humongous:巨大无比的
backlash:强烈反应,对抗性反应

杀手汽车

要是让我选个第二职业，我想写汽车广告。再好点，我想生活在汽车广告所营造的生活中。

在现实生活中，你、我在写错了名字的高速公路上蜗牛般爬行，还不时焦急地按响喇叭。可是在商业广告的神话王国中，驾车者却能在绿树成荫的公路上尽享驾车的乐趣，如入无人之境。

我们在城市的街道上走走停停，但那个驾驶着雷克萨斯的家伙却处在"第一跑道"——一段盘绕摩天大楼而上的高架路。我们在街区来回打转，只是为了找个停车位，但是丰田四轮驱动休闲运动车的车主居然能将车停放在开阔的沙滩上。我们在隧道里遭遇塞车，但是凯雷德却可以在空旷的大街上大摇大摆地前进，因为"这里没有路障"。

汽车广告向通勤的人所传递的信息与万宝路广告向癌症病人所传递的思想简直有异曲同工之效。

这一切不过是向各地通勤的人大肆吹嘘的前奏曲：来辆运动型多功能汽车吧。是的，就是那些高速公路上横行霸道的、耗油的、侵占停车位的大块头。

购买这些运动型多功能汽车的人最喜欢的运动是"血拼"，他们最常参加的体育项目就是载着孩子去参加美式足球训练。

运动型多功能汽车的块头和销售量的增长速度让我联想到了国防预算。在军备竞争日益激烈的今天，人们购买运动型多功能汽车也是出于自我防卫的目的。防备什么呢？当然是其他的运动型多功能汽车了。

我在这些庞然大物的阴影中遭遇了多次塞车，也自然就对由它们所导致的每年2000多人的死亡不觉奇怪了。如果重达6000磅的雪佛兰巨无霸与一辆1800磅的公交车相撞,那么吃亏的一定是公交车。如果公交车撞了巨无霸,吃亏的也还是公交车。

运动型多功能汽车的问题在于你光是看着它们可不行,你必须对它们时刻保持警惕。并不只有我一个小车车主在这些大块头轰轰开过时有种危机感。它们的"彪悍"行径促使南加州的汽车俱乐部向运动型多功能汽车车主提出一条建议:"抛开'公路战士'的情结。有些车主有种错觉,认为他们能够不理会各种规章而横冲直撞。"

然而,最大、最棘手的问题还不只是安全问题,它们也威胁着我们的环境。时至今日,法律还在纵容运动型多功能汽车造成两倍、三倍于其他机动车的污染。在郊区,很多有"良知"的人士开着每15英里消耗1加仑汽油的大家伙,就只为到市郊回收中心送几个空瓶子。也有一些父母为确保孩子的人身安全一掷千金买回辆庞然大物,可是孩子们吸入的却是被污染的空气。

现在,终于出台了一些小措施。美国环保署首次提议把运动型多功能汽车等同于普通汽车来对待。如果可能,巨无霸的尾气排放量不得超过福特金牛座。这是一个重要的开始,但还远远不够。

以福特车为例。汽车制造商生产出相对清洁的发动机。但是,今年秋天他们却要推出无比巨大的"旅行者"。它身高7英尺、80英寸宽,重达4吨,在城市中每行走10英里耗油1加仑。难怪塞拉俱乐部把它称作"福特瓦尔迪兹港"。开这车送孩子去上学不错——如果你担心在路上遭遇坦克的话。

尽管我也曾希望坐在运动型多功能汽车中去兜兜风,体验保险杠与挡风玻璃在同一视线的感觉,但是我还不至于那样。自从汽车没有了尾翼以来,运动型多功能汽车风头太劲,即便它能彰显尊贵,但是却不为社会所看好。

在偏远的地方拥有一辆运动型多功能汽车是一回事,而开着它进城则是另一回事。最后,这个大块头最好的归宿就是汽车广告了。因为在那里,天总是晴朗的,驾驶者总是惬意轻松的,而且视线之内永远也没有第二

辆车。

More to Read

美国是一个汽车文化非常发达的国家。二战之后,美国的汽车突然大了起来,经历了二战的人们有一种死里逃生的感觉,他们要铺张,要今朝有酒今朝醉,在这种心态畸变下诞生了宽大的美国汽车,折射出了二战之后人们那种绝地重生的感觉。此外还有一个原因是,美国地大物博,人们崇尚自由、宽松,所以美国人对"SUV"极其钟情。但是,"SUV"的迅猛发展也不可避免地带来了很多问题,让人们又爱又恨。

透视 PERCEPTION

Reading Guidance

　　作者从法国巴黎跳探戈舞的朋友开始，一直写到了布拉格，让读者感受到了7月欧洲欢乐而美好的氛围。之后，他笔锋一转，将读者的思绪引到了大洋彼岸的美国。虽然，新大陆和旧大陆在文化上同宗同源，但是在对待生活和工作的态度上差别很明显。作者从价值观上找到了这种差异的根源。作者写这篇文章的目的是唤醒美国民众对生活乐趣的关注，隐晦地批判了流行于美国的"拼命工作、尽情玩乐"的理念和美国人日渐膨胀的物质占有欲。或许，工作和乐趣不能够截然分开，何不像欧洲人那样淡定、从容些？

Europeans Just Want to Have Fun

　　Long vocations. Lots of dancing. So why can't we loosen up?

　　Walking across Boulevard St. Michel, in Paris last week, on the night before Bastille Day, I bumped into an old friend—an American who has lived in the city for 25 years who told me he was taking up the tango. When I asked him why, he suggested I take a stroll along the Left Bank of the Siege, opposite Le St. Louis, and so of course I did.

⟨161⟩

It was one big party. A crowd was tangoing away in a makeshift, open-air amphitheater. Nearby, a multiethnic group was doing the merengue. Hundreds of others were tucking into picnics by the river as a full moon rose in a cloudless sky. Much later that night, after a perfect fish soup in the Place des Vosges, I walked into the narrow passages of the Marais district and stumbled upon an impromptu block party. Someone had set up a sound system on the sidewalk, and the street was packed with people—straight and gay, young and old, black and white—dancing to salsa.

Europe is enjoying itself. OK, in late July, it always does. The weekend I was in Paris, an estimated 500,000 kids descended on Berlin for the annual Love Parade, a carnival of techno music. Meanwhile, tens of thousands of families started their treks from the damp north of the continent to their vacation homes in the warm south. But even when the sun isn't shining, Europeans seem to be throwing themselves into fun and festivity with unprecedented zeal. Each weekend, central London is one great bacchanal. Cities that for reasons of politics or religion were once gloomily repressive—Madrid, say, or Dublin—now rock to the small hours. In Prague the foreign visitor who get talked about are not the earnest young Americans who flocked there in the early 1990s, but British partygoers who have flown in for the cheap beer and pretty girls. The place that British historian Mark Mazower once called the true dark continent—and from whose soul the horrors of fascism sprang—has become a community at play.

Funny. This is how the U. S. was supposed to be. In a famous series of essays collected in his 1976 book, *The Cultural Contradictions of Capitalism*, Daniel Bell noted how the decline of the Protestant small-town ethic had unhinged American capitalism form its moral foundation in the intrinsic value of work. By the 1960, Bell argues, "the cultural justification of capitalism (had) become unprecedented, the idea of pleasure as a way of life." In a 1969 cover story tilted *California*: *A State of Excitement*, *Time* reported that, as most Americans saw it, "'the good, godless, gregarious pursuit of pleasure is what California is all about... I have seen the future.' says the newly returned visitor to California."

But the American future didn't turn out as we expected. While Europeans cut the hours they spend at the office or factory—in France it is illegal to work more than 35 hours a week—and lengthened their vacations, Americans were concluding that you could be happy only if you work hard and play hard. So they began to stay at their jobs longer than ever and then, in jam-packed weekends at places like the Hampton on Long Island, invented the uniquely American concept of scheduled joy, filling a day off with one appointment after another, as if it were no different from one at the office. American conservatives, meanwhile, came to believe that Europeans' desire to devote themselves to the pleasures of life and—the shame of it—six weeks annual vacation was evidence of a lack of seriousness and would, in any event, end in economic tears.

Why do Europeans and Americans differ so much in their attitude toward work and leisure? I can think of two reasons. First, the crowded confines of Western Europe and the expansive space of North America have led to varied consumer preferences. Broadly speaking, Americans value stuff—SUVs, 7,000 square feet houses—more than they value time, while for Europeans it's the opposite. Second, as Bell predicted, America's sense of itself as a religious nation has revived. At least in the puritanical version of Christianity that has always appealed to Americans, religion comes packaged with the stern message that hard work is good for the soul. Modern Europe has avoided so melancholy a lesson.

Whatever the explanation, the idea of a work-life balance is a staple of European discourse, studied in think tanks, proposed by policymakers. In the U.S., the term, when it's used at all, is said with the sort of sneer reserved for those who eat quiche. But it might still catch on. When Bill Keller was named executive editor of the *New York Times* last week, he encouraged the staff to do "a little more savoring" of life, spending time with their families or viewing art. Even better, they could take up the tango.

Notes

tuck:把……塞进
impromptu:即兴的
unprecedented:前所未有的
bacchanal:酒神节
savor:品尝

及时行乐在欧洲

  欧洲人喜欢放长假和跳舞。而我们为什么就不能过轻松的生活呢?
  法国国庆节前夜,穿过巴黎米歇尔林荫大道时,我偶遇一个在巴黎住了25年的老友。他告诉我最近他开始学习探戈了。当我询问原因时,他建议我到塞纳河左岸对着圣路易斯的地方去看看。于是我就去了。
  那真是一个盛大的派对啊。一群人在临时的露天圆形剧场跳着探戈。附近还有许多不同民族的人聚在一起在跳梅伦格。满月挂在繁星点点的天空,许多人在河边享受美味野餐。我在浮日广场享用味道绝美的鱼汤时已经是深夜了。但当我穿过玛黑区的小巷时,偶然间又发现了一个即兴的街区聚会。有人在人行道上安装了音响设备,街上挤满了人——异性恋者和同性恋者,青年和老人,黑人和白人——他们正在跳萨尔萨。
  欧洲人过得真快活,每年7月末,都是这样的。我在巴黎的那个周末,大约50万孩子聚集在柏林,参加一年一度的爱之旅。与此同时,大多数家庭开始了度假旅程,离开寒冷的大陆北部来到温暖的南方度假屋。即使阳光并不明媚,欧洲人也会以极大的热情投入到娱乐和狂欢中去。伦敦的每个周末都宛如酒神节。曾因政治和宗教原因而倍感压抑的马德里人和都柏林人,现在也能狂欢到凌晨。在布拉格遭人非议的不是20世纪90年代初成群结队、热情洋溢的美国小伙,而是为了廉价啤酒和美女而飞来这里的英国派对迷。这个曾被英国历史学家马克·马佐尔称为"真正黑暗的大陆"、崇拜法西斯主义的地方,如今已经成为了一个人间天堂。

可笑啊,本应该是美国人过这样的日子才对。丹尼尔·贝尔在其1976年的专著《资本主义文化矛盾论》中指责新教徒狭隘的道德观混淆了美国资本主义道德基础中关于工作的内在价值。贝尔指出:"20世纪60年代,人们把资本主义定义为享乐主义,活着就是为了享乐。"1969年,《时代周刊》的封面故事《加州:激动人心的地方》描述道:"很多刚从加州回来的人都认为,'加州是享乐主义者的天堂……未来全美国都会这样的……肯定会这样的'。"

但是,美国的未来却和我们想象的不一样。当欧洲人缩短工时,延长假期的时候(在法国,每周工作超过35个小时是违法的),美国人却得出结论,拼命工作、尽情玩乐,生活才会快乐。于是,他们就比任何时期都努力工作,而后在类似长岛的汉普顿这样的景点度过繁忙的周末;他们发明出只有美国人能想出的"有时限快乐"这种概念,周末就在一个接一个的约会中度过,与上班时并无二致。同时,美国保守主义者认为"欧洲人决意贪图享乐,简直是给自己蒙羞。每年六个礼拜的假期是一种对生活的不敬,他们早晚会因为经济衰退而号啕大哭"。

为什么欧洲人和美国人在关于工作和休息问题上的分歧这么大呢?我想原因有两个。第一,西欧疆域狭窄,美国领土广袤,因此形成了不同的消费倾向。大体上说,美国人认为拥有运动型轿车和7000平方英尺的房子比有闲更重要,而欧洲人则恰恰相反。第二,如同贝尔所说,美国的"宗教国家"观念复活了。宗教总是充斥着苛刻的要求,受美国大众喜爱的清教教义中有这样的内容:努力工作有益灵魂。然而,现代欧洲尽量回避这

种令人感伤的理念。

　　工作和生活保持平衡是欧洲人关心的话题,也是政治智囊团所研究、决策者所思考的生活观。美国人一提到这些,总是很不屑。但是,美国人的想法有一天可能也会改变。上周被任命为《纽约时报》总编的比尔·凯勒就职时还鼓励员工们要"多些时间品味生活",比如陪陪家人、看看画展。

　　跳探戈当然是个更好的选择。

More to Read

　　在作者看来,美国人更看重运动型跑车和7000平方英尺的大房子。美国人对于物质主义的追捧是其文化的一个侧面。在美国,个人成就往往被打上物质的烙印,这使得成功变得易于衡量,也易于被人所察。因此,在美国人看来,社会的进步所指的便是学校数量的多少而不是教学质量的优劣、师资水平的高低。对于有形成绩的追求让美国人在很多主要问题的判断上有失准确。理解了这一点,我们也就明白为什么"有闲"没有大房子来得重要。"有闲"在美国人看来似乎跟无所事事是同义词,甚至从某种程度上说,只有失业的人才会这样。

透视 PERCEPTION

Reading Guidance

本文为我们讲述了一杯香浓的咖啡背后的故事。咖啡文化并不像我们认为的那样在老牌资本主义国家诞生的,而是在也门这样一个小国家诞生的。咖啡文化的兴起与咖啡馆的出现是密不可分的,可以说咖啡馆就是咖啡文化的摇篮。人们来到咖啡馆,不仅仅是要品尝一杯上好的咖啡,更重要的是进行社交,谈天说地,议论时局。因此,咖啡馆的命运也与政治发展联系在了一起,或兴或衰,或荣或损。

Keeping Up With Coffee Culture

What's the coffee culture like in your city? Coffee culture, a term that Wikipedia defines as "a term used to describe a social atmosphere that depends heavily on coffee shops, espresso in particular, as a social lubricant". The truth is that coffee culture has existed for centuries, and the popularity of coffee shops in the late 1900s is just another little bubble in the history of coffee culture throughout the world.

The earliest record of coffee culture dates to the early 1400s in Yemen, one of the earliest exporters of coffee. The tradition of coffee houses, on which the establishment of a coffee culture depends, began in Mecca, and was encouraged by those in power who felt that the influence of coffee was better than that of another popular stimulant, kat. Those coffee houses were called kaveh kanes, and became social hubs where men could gather over coffee to discuss business, exchange gossip, play chess and enjoy entertainment—all for the price of a cup of coffee. Sounds an awful lot like the coffee shops and coffee culture of today, no? The Yemeni coffee houses were also places where politics were discussed and rebellion fomented, which eventually led to their attempted suppression—not once, not twice, but repeatedly. The coffee culture was so entrenched by this time, though, that it proved nearly impossible to eradicate the coffee houses. Instead, the government eventually cashed in on the trend by taxing coffee by the cup. Much later, a Dutch traveler noted about the coffee culture in Yemen that the coffee houses were "the only theatres for the exercise of (non-religious) eloquence. Young scholars walk about and deliver discourses on all sorts of subjects. They make up the most wonderful tales, inventing, singing, making tales and fables". The manuscript, written by Carsten Niebuhr in the 1760s, sounds remarkably like an open mike reading at a coffee house today.

Between the beginnings of coffee houses in Yemen and Niebuhr's visit there, though, coffee culture had started to spread throughout the world. By 1475, there are written records of a coffee house called Kiva Han in Constantinople. Turkish coffee, brewed in an ibrik, was served along with entertainment and—no surprise—political and social commentary. The first recorded coffee house in Europe was, interestingly, the result of the spoils of war. The story of that first cafe is possibly one of the most romantic in the annals of coffee culture. The Turkish armies had encamped in Vienna, taking over the city. A young Pole by the name of Franz Georg Kolschitzky, had been instrumental in engineering the defeat of the Turkish. He and a servant slipped into the Turkish encampment and wandered around it, gathering information that he then carried with him to the Christian troops of King Sobieski and Duke Charles of Lorraine.

His message brought the troops to Constantinople just in time to save the city. When asked to name his reward for his service, Kolschitzky asked for 500 pounds of 'camel fodder' that had been left behind by the Turks. Using that camel fodder—green coffee beans—Kolschitzky established Vienna's first coffee house, Kolschitzky's Cafe.

Coffee culture spread throughout Europe quickly and made its way to the British isles. Between 1670 and 1685, coffee houses sprouted up throughout London, attracting scholars and politicians. Writing in 1675, a young man noted.

"Now, whither shall a person, wearied with hard study, or the laborious turmoil of a tedious day, repair to refresh himself? Or where can young gentlemen, or shopkeepers, more innocently and advantageously spend an hour or two in the evening, than at a coffee house? Where they shall be sure to meet company, and, by the custom of the house, not such as at other places, stingy and reserved to themselves, but free and communicative; where every man may modestly begin his story, and propose to, or answer another, as he thinks fit... In brief, it is undeniable, that, as you have here the most civil, so it is, generally, the most intelligent society."

Nearly 350 years ago, the unnamed scholar described what is still the dominant coffee culture in coffee houses throughout the world—a place where people come to spend an hour or two, meet company, tell stories and entertain each other. Coffee culture revolved around entertainment, erudition and politics. In London, the coffee houses were nicknamed "penny universities", where a man could learn more in an evening of listening than he could in a month of studying. In 1675, King Charles II tried to ban coffee houses as "hotbeds of revolution", but had to withdraw his proclamation after just 11 days because of the public outcry against it. The coffee culture was so entrenched and involved that it birthed other innovations in society. Jonathan's Coffee House in Change Alley, for instance, was the birthplace of the London Stock Exchange, and Edward Lloyd's Coffee House eventually became the headquarters for Lloyds of

London, still the world's most famous insurance company.

Today, the general impression of the coffee culture is not much different than it was back in Yemen and Constantinople in the 1400s and 1500s. Coffee houses are congenial places where people meet, exchange ideas, listen to storytellers, enjoy art and entertain each other. While the big chains spread across the world, independent coffee shops continue to offer more than a fix of espresso—they offer a heady shot of coffee culture well-mixed with company, political discourse and a chance to mingle with others who are as enchanted by the atmosphere as they are the bean.

Notes

lubricant：润滑剂
stimulant：兴奋剂
eloquence：雄辩

咖啡文化寻源

你所在城市里的咖啡文化是什么样的？咖啡文化，在维基百科中的定义是"描述一种依赖咖啡馆，特别是意式咖啡馆而产生的社会气氛的词汇，就像一种社会润滑剂"。事实上，咖啡文化已经存在了数百年。20 世纪初期咖啡店的流行，只不过是全世界咖啡文化在历史上的一个小小的缩影。

关于咖啡文化的最早记录可追溯到 15 世纪的也门，那里是最早的咖啡出口地之一。作为咖啡文化载体的咖啡屋最初见于穆哈。当时的掌权者认为咖啡的兴奋作用比另一种流行的兴奋剂"开特"要强,于是鼓励将其推广。那时的咖啡屋被称为"kaveh kanes",并逐渐成为人们边喝咖啡边谈生意、闲聊、下棋、取乐的中心——只需买上一杯咖啡,便能得到上述许多乐趣。这听起来跟今天的咖啡店和咖啡文化惊人的相似,不是吗?也门的咖啡屋也是谈论政治和煽动叛乱的地方,这最终酿成了咖啡屋被禁的命运,而且不是一次两次那么简单。然而那时咖啡文化已深入人心,要将咖啡馆根除几乎是不可能的。但政府最终通过向每一杯咖啡征税达到了目的。很久以后,一位荷兰旅行者注意到了也门的咖啡文化,他指出"咖啡馆是(非宗教)演说的唯一场所。年轻的学者走来走去,对任何话题都表示悲观。他们捏造谎言、四处告密,编造故事和神话,自己却成了最传奇的故事"。这段话虽出自卡尔斯顿·尼布尔18世纪60年代的手稿,但又何尝不是现代咖啡馆文化的真实写照?

咖啡屋在也门出现后,咖啡文化早在尼布尔到访之前就已经在世界各地传播了。1475年,君士坦丁堡已有了关于名为"大圆堡"(Kiva Han)的咖啡馆的文字记录。土耳其咖啡由土耳其铜壶煮泡而成,喝咖啡的同时还有娱乐活动,如果不出所料的话,期间也少不了政治和社会评论。有意思的是,在欧洲,有史记载的第一家咖啡馆竟是战利品的功劳。关于这个咖啡馆的故事有可能是咖啡文化史上最浪漫的故事之一。土耳其军队在维也纳扎营后,占领了这座城市。一位叫科尔舍斯基的荷兰年轻人为抵抗土耳其军队做出了重要贡献。他带着一个仆人溜到土耳其军营后面四处打探,搜集情报,然后将情报交给索伯斯基国王的基督教军队和洛林的查尔斯公爵。他的情报将军队及时地带到君士坦丁堡,解救了维也纳。当被问道想要什么作为犒赏时,科尔舍斯基要了土耳其军溃逃时扔下的500磅"骆驼饲料"——绿色的咖啡豆——科尔舍斯基建立了维也纳的第一家咖啡馆——科尔舍斯基咖啡馆。

咖啡文化在欧洲迅速蔓延,最终到达英伦三岛。在1670至1685年之间,咖啡馆在伦敦接二连三地出现,吸引着学者和政客。1675年,一位年轻人写道:"现在,一个人无论是因沉重学业而疲惫不堪,还是因整天劳动而筋疲力尽,会怎样令自己振作起来呢?当一位年轻的绅士或一位店主想要在晚上消磨一两个小时,什么地方比一间咖啡馆更便利呢?如果人们想要在一个能使人慷慨且敞开心扉的地方,而不是一个让人吝啬而有所保留的地方跟朋友见面,他们会选在哪里呢?有哪个地方能让任何一个人都畅所欲言,并且对别人的问题直言不讳呢?总之不可否认,咖啡馆是最富有文化气息的地方,也是公认的最活跃的社交场所。"

这位不知名的学者在大约350年前所描述的咖啡文化至今仍统治着世界各地的咖啡馆——一个人们可以消磨时光,会见商业伙伴,讲述故事,相互取悦的地方。咖啡文化与娱乐、学识和政治是密不可分的。在伦敦,咖啡馆被戏称为"便士大学",一个人在咖啡馆一个晚上听到的东西比他一个月所学到的知识都多。1675年,查尔斯二世试图以"革命温床"的名义关闭咖啡馆,但因为群众的公开抗议,不得不于11天后就撤销了法令。咖啡文化如此深入人心,甚至成了社会上其他新生事物的根基。例如,位于零钱胡同的乔纳斯坦咖啡馆,是伦敦股票交易所的诞生地。爱德华·劳埃德咖啡馆最终成为伦敦劳合社的总部,至今仍是世界上最著名的保险公司。

今天,咖啡文化的大致概念与15世纪在也门、16世纪在君士坦丁堡没有太大分别。咖啡馆仍是人们会见朋友、交流思想、聆听故事、欣赏艺术以及互相取悦时所中意的场所。当庞大的咖啡连锁店在全球蔓延时,独立的咖啡馆仍继续供应着比一杯意式特浓咖啡更深刻的东西——他们提供了一种让人振奋的咖啡文化——友谊、政治探讨,以及与那些被咖啡馆的气氛所迷醉而认为自己就是咖啡豆的人深入交流的机会。

More to Read

咖啡文化的发展历程真是曲折。幸好,它的生命力比较顽强,虽曾屡遭打击和排斥,但最终还是留在了历史的舞台上,并在现代生活中继续扮演着重要角色。不然,我们的生活中又少了一个可以互诉衷肠、读书看报的地方。现在,请掩上书卷,喝一杯咖啡,温习我们刚刚讲过的故事。

透视 PERCEPTION

Reading Guidance

　　本文以轻松、调侃的方式讲述了作者在巴黎的一些见闻。因为是巴黎之旅,文中出现了一些法语表达。大家不妨在阅读英语的同时,也试着接触些法语——这门号称"世界最美的语言"。其实,英语和法语有很深的渊源,英语中的很多表达来自于法语,所以如果读者英语基础比较扎实,那么面对一些法语文章倒还不至于"目不识丁"。在文中,"Un verre de vin rouge, s'il vous plait"是"请给我一杯红酒";"manger et boire trop"是"吃和喝得很多";"VIVE LA FRANCE"是"法兰西万岁"。感兴趣的读者不妨把这几句法语试着翻译成英语吧!此外,文中的很多美食名称也是地道的法语,大家可以参照一下后面的中文译文,不要忘了英语中的很多美食的名称就是直接的"拿来主义",它们的故乡就在法国,比如"baguette"(法国长面包、法棍)、"croissant"(牛角或羊角包)、"omelette"(煎蛋饼)等。

An English Girl in Paris

　　There are many reasons to visit Paris: to tour the galleries, go shopping in designer boutiques or just to be in the city of love. However, in all honesty, my main motive for crossing the channel is simply for the wine and the cheese. I, an English girl, am going to tell you what to eat, where to eat and reveal

whether France can hold onto its seat at the head of the dining table...

The French are good at three things: making cheese, making wine and going on strike. Yes, Oliver may have been extolling the best of British culinary delights in *Food, Glorious Food*, but nothing beats French cuisine. But as Bob Dylan knows all too well, the times they are a-changin' and France no longer trumps everyone else's attempts at good food, with the New World wines becoming more popular with drinkers and connoisseurs alike. Should France be worried? Perhaps not just yet, as they still have plenty to offer the average foodie...

First, let's talk about the booze. "Un verre de vin rouge, s'il vous plait" is fast becoming my most used phrase over here. This may have something to do with my burgeoning alcoholic status, but is also to do with the fact that cheap wine is so bloody lovely over here. Back home, the cheapest you can get is around the £4 mark, and that's barely drinkable. Here, some of the best wine I've had has been under three Euro and from the petrol station round the corner. Oh yes, we keep it classy on the Rive Gauche.

When in Paris, do as the Parisians do and embrace the café culture. The French have made a sport out of people-watching and are unashamedly obvious about it as all tables face out onto the pavement. Oui, a small café crème may cost you more than five times what it would cost to make at home, but you're not paying for the coffee, you're paying to spy on passers-by. That's why it's cheaper inside. The French are weird in that prices go up depending on where you are in the establishment—don't expect a seat if you're paying less than three Euro for a coffee. On the other hand, four Euro or more will get you that prime spot to people-watch and be watched. Brasseries and bistros are also part of the culture and easy on the wallet too, great for filling food and a pleasant atmosphere.

In my quest to inform and entertain you, dear reader, I have sampled some of the more peculiar French specialities and can tell you that snails mainly taste of the garlic butter they are cooked in, with a distinctly rubbery and bobbly texture.

So, what plats would I recommend? Tartiflette, a cheesy carb feast that helps kick a hangover, a still-bleeding steak accompanied by some thin frites, a freshly baked baguette and camembert, a cracking croque monsieur or madame and all of the pastries and gateaux available… And the macaroons… ooh the macaroons… Veggies and vegans beware however: France is not the best place for you. Not only do the restaurants and cafés hardly cater for you, but also it is very difficult to come by meat-replacements such as Quorn. However, head for the Marais district or the Latin Quarter around the Panthéon, and you're sure to find something to suit.

Considering how much I've been stuffing my face with treats since I've been here, it seems a miracle that I've actually lost weight. Well, I guess the absence of lifts everywhere does have an upside. Living in a country where you can manger et boire trop and still lose inches off your waistline? VIVE LA FRANCE!

Notes

booze：酒
burgeoning：迅速成长的
hangover：宿醉
vegan：纯素主义者（既不吃也不用任何动物产品，如蛋、丝绸、皮革）

英国女孩的巴黎之旅

到巴黎去的理由很多：参观美术馆，在高级服装店里购物，或者只是在浪漫的"爱之都"浸淫些时日……然而，坦率地讲，我漂洋过海来到巴黎，主要目的是品红酒，尝奶酪。我——来自英国的女孩——这就来告诉您巴黎最好吃的是什么，怎么吃；我还想让您看看法国是否能保住其餐桌霸主的宝座。

法国人擅长三件事：做奶酪、酿红酒和罢工。诚然，奥利弗在《美食，了不起的美食》一书中曾大赞英国美食，但是其中无一能与法国烹饪媲美。但是正如鲍勃·迪伦所深知的那样，我们的时代日新月异，不断变化。法国在制作美食的尝试上也不再是一枝独秀。来自新大陆的红酒越来越受欢迎，连品酒家都爱不释手。法国应该为此担忧吗？也许现在还不必过虑，因为她还有大量美食来款待普通的美食家呢。

首先，让我们谈谈酒吧。"请来一杯红酒！"是我在这里说得最多的一句话，都快成口头禅了。这也许是因为我越来越嗜酒，但不容忽视的事实是巴黎廉价酒的口感都极其正点。在英国，最便宜的红酒每杯也要4英镑，但是那酒简直难以下咽。在这里，即便是在街角加油站买来的酒都很好喝，价钱却还不到3欧元。哦，对了，这个价位在塞纳河左岸是最贵的了。

到了巴黎，就得入乡随俗，像巴黎人一样热情拥抱这里的咖啡馆文化。法国人发明了一种运动——观赏人来人往，他们可以毫不避讳地看个够，因为咖啡馆里所有的餐桌都是面向人行道的。咖啡馆里出售的奶油咖啡的价钱是家中自制咖啡成本的五倍。但是，咱可不是在为咖啡埋单，咱是在掏钱偷窥形形色色的路人甲和路人乙呢。正因为如此，咖啡馆里面的座位要便宜很多。法国人很怪,花钱多少完全取决于你在咖啡馆中的"地理位置"!要是只点一杯不到 3 欧元的咖啡,就不要妄想有座了,只有"站票"咯。不过,要是你愿意花上 4 欧元,就足可以占尽地利——不仅自己可以一饱眼福,也能让人一睹你的风采。啤酒馆和小餐馆也是法国文化的一部分,而且在那些地方不用花太多钱就可以坐拥优美的环境,尽享可口的美食。

亲爱的读者们,为了让你们既长知识又开心,我还亲自品尝了一些法国特色美食。我可以告诉你,所谓焗蜗牛就只是带着蒜味和黄油香味的口感还不错的圆柱状弹性物质而已。

那我会向您推荐什么呢?奶酪土豆洋葱熏肉塔,它可是能解酒的哦。还有血淋淋的牛排、刚烤好的法棍面包、卡蒙贝尔芝士奶酪、法式火腿奶酪吐司、各种各样的馅饼、奶油蛋糕……还有蛋白杏仁饼干……美味的蛋白杏仁饼干……不过提醒素食主义者和纯素主义者:法国不是你们的最佳选择。餐馆和咖啡馆不但不提供素食,连植物素肉这样的肉类代替品都不容易找到。然而,在历史悠久的玛黑区或者先贤祠附近的拉丁居住区,你倒是能找到满意的答案。

算算我在巴黎塞进嘴里的那些东西吧,我没胖反瘦真可谓是奇迹了。我想所到之处少有电梯还是有些好处的。在哪个国家你既能胡吃海喝还能减掉腰部的赘肉呢?法兰西万岁!

More to Read

正如作者所言,我们有太多游览巴黎的理由。可是,在这里作者并没有为我们展示香榭丽舍大街琳琅满目的商品,也没有赘述埃菲尔铁塔的气势恢弘,更没有把卢浮宫里令人叹为观止的稀世珍宝一一放大。或许,官方的介绍早已让人耳膜生茧;又或许,此般的巴黎太高高在上,容易让人产生距离感。反倒是日常生活中的柴米油盐、一杯咖啡、一杯红酒、一片面包更能让人自然、自在地融入她,而忘记自己"身在异乡为异客"。吃吃喝喝又何尝不是一种品位?也难怪法国人的幸福指数如此之高。读着读着,真的是"身未动,心已远"了!

Reading Guidance

欧内斯特·米勒·海明威（Ernest Miller Hemingway），美国小说家，代表作有《老人与海》、《太阳照样升起》、《永别了，武器》、《丧钟为谁而鸣》等，他凭借《老人与海》获得1953年的普利策奖及1954年的诺贝尔文学奖。海明威被誉为美利坚民族的精神丰碑，并且是"新闻体"小说的创始人，他的写作风格以简洁著称，1930年，海明威发表过一篇论述西班牙斗牛的文章，以此为基础，两年后他写成了《午后之死》一书。在书中他对斗牛作了极为详尽而有趣的介绍，指出斗牛是一种"艺术家处于生命危险之中的绝无仅有的艺术"，并从斗牛引申开去，论及了小说创作的一些理论和具体原则，以及他对死亡的深刻见解。想知道究竟什么是斗牛，它的具体过程如何，它对社会经济起到什么样的作用，它的美学意义究竟何在，它对人的自尊与勇气又会是什么样的考验，那么，这本书就非读不可。然而，《午后之死》一书的价值或重要性绝不仅于此。

Death in the Afternoon:
Hemingway Now Writes of Bull-Fighting as an Art

The emergence of Mr. Hemingway as an authority on bull-fighting should not be a surprise to anyone who has read the passages in *The Sun Also Rises* which touch upon that peculiarly Latin sport. That he is an authority may be

透视 PERCEPTION

conceded, even by those who have never seen a matador, not only from Mr. Hemingway's statement that he has seen fifteen hundred bulls killed on the field of honor and his acknowledgment of indebtedness to some 2,077 books and pamphlets in Spanish dealing with, but from the internal evidence of the book itself.

One would say that Mr. Hemingway knows bull-fighting at least as well as the specialized sports writer in our own country knows baseball, football, racing or fighting. He knows it so well that on occasion only the introduction of an extremely singular old lady as the author's interlocutor, a few digressions on death, modern literature and sex life, joined with Mr. Hemingway's extremely masculine style of writing, save the reader from drowning in a flood of technicalities.

It may be asked why Mr. Hemingway should infer in American readers a sufficiently passionate interest in bull-fighting to induce them to buy and read a book of 517 pages on the subject. But this would be to put the cart before the horse—or letting the bull wave a red cloth at the matador instead of vice versa. Bull-fighting, one infers, became a hobby with Mr. Hemingway because of the light it throws on Spain, on human nature and on life and death. In a sense this book is Mr. Hemingway's book on "Virgin Spain". The reference is pertinent because, as he explains in an extremely candid bit of analysis, Mr. Hemingway does not particularly like that style of writing for which his most flattering epithet is "bedside mysticism". But the author's fundamental motive is perhaps this:

"The only place where you could see life and death, i. e., violent death now that the wars were over, was in the bull ring and I wanted very much to go to Spain where I could study it. I was trying to learn to write, commencing with the simplest things, and one of the simplest things of all and the most fundamental is violent death."

In another passage Mr. Hemingway points out that one of the essentials if a country is to love bull-fights is "that the people must have an interest in death". The people of Castile, he finds, have such an interest in death, "and when they can see it being given, avoided, refused and accepted in the afternoon for a nominal price of admission they pay their money and go to the bullring". The English and French, on the other hand, "live for life" and consequently don't especially care for bull-fights. Here Mr. Hemingway seems to be getting mystical on his own account, but at least it is not "bedside mysticism".

Bull-fighting always means death for the bull, for if he is not killed in the arena during the allotted time he is killed outside. It means death for horses—a death in which Mr. Hemingway says there is sometimes an element of the comic—if they are not protected by mattresses. It sometimes means death for the matador, it means in almost every case that he will sooner other later be grievously wounded, and if he is a good matador it means that he must go to the very brink of death every time he puts on a performance. Moreover, it means that a good matador must actually enjoy killing and that the spectators must be able to derive an emotional kick from the operation. As Mr. Hemingway puts it:

"He (the matador) must have a spiritual enjoyment of the moment of killing. Killing cleanly and in a way which gives you esthetic pleasure and pride has always been one of the greatest enjoyments of a part of the human race. Once you accept the rule of death thou shalt not kill is an easily and naturally obeyed commandment. But when a man is still in rebellion against death he has pleasure in taking to himself one of the Godlike attributes, that of giving it. This is one of the most profound feelings in those men who enjoy killing. These things are done in pride and pride, of course, is a Christian sin and a pagan virtue. But it is pride which makes the bull-fight and true enjoyment of killing which makes the great matador."

The "true enjoyment" of the fan or "aficionado" is in the bravery or "nobility" of the bull and in the skill and bravery of the matador. At least these are the points upon which Mr. Hemingway dwells. The "aficionado" does not want to see a good matador killed, though he may be indifferent to the wounding of a bad matador, or even try to damage him a little by hurling bottles and other hard objects at him as he leaves the ring. But it is hard to believe that those to whom death is of profound interest may not sometimes hope that if a matador is to be killed by a bull they may be there to see it. And Mr. Hemingway does make it clear that the nearer the matador comes to the horns at the supreme moment the better liked his performance is. The bull ring is not the place for skill without risk. As a confirmed bull-fight fan Mr. Hemingway is disgusted with a matador who kills by a trick, stroke "bulls that he is supposed to expose his body to in killing with the sword". If the finishing thrust is properly put in, the matador must always be in such a position that if a gust of wind comes at the wrong time or if the bull suddenly raises his head the man will be gored. If no part of the spectators feels any morbid expectation at such crises a Spanish assemblage is different from other gatherings.

But bull-fighting is an art. It does not seem absurd to Mr. Hemingway to compare it with sculpture and painting. Even such refined elements as the line of the matador's body at the critical instant or the "composition" of bull and man enter into the intelligent "aficionado's" enjoyment. Bull-fighting is thus presented as an art heightened by the presence of death and, if the spectator can project himself into the matador's place, in the terror of death. For even the best matadors have their moments of fear—even their days and seasons of fear.

The book is thus not only a careful, even a meticulous explanation of the way bull-fighting is done, but is also a picturing of the spirit in which it is done and seen.

It may be said flatly that the famous Hemingway style is neither so clear nor so forceful in most passages of *Death in the Afternoon* as it is in his novels and short stories. In this book Mr. Hemingway is guilty of the grievous sin of writing sentences which have to be read two or three times before the meaning is clear.

The book will certainly find its place on the shelves of Hemingway addicts.

Notes

sufficiently：充足地
matador：斗牛士
candid：率直的
grievous：严重的

《午后之死》
——海明威与斗牛艺术

　　海明威先生现在成了斗牛权威了。这对曾经读过《太阳照样升起》的读者来说并不稀奇,在那本小说中海明威已经开始关注斗牛这项具有拉丁风情的运动了。即使是从未见过斗牛士的人也得承认海明威的确很权威,不仅是因为海明威说他曾经亲眼见证过 1500 头牛血染斗牛场或者读了 2077 份有关斗牛的西班牙语书籍和宣传册,更重要的是他书里的那些内容,真可谓言之凿凿。

　　你可能会说海明威先生对斗牛了如指掌,与我们国家那些专门从事棒球、橄榄球、赛马或搏斗的体育评论员不相上下。他驾轻就熟地把一个不同寻常的老妪、逃避死亡、现代文学、情爱之事这些元素与他的硬汉写作风格相结合,以使读者从繁杂的创作技巧中解脱出来而获得更多阅读享受。

　　你可能会问,海明威何以能让他对斗牛的热情感染美国读者而使他们心甘情愿地去买这本 517 页厚的书来读。不过这个问题有点本末倒置,就像是让牛向斗牛士挥舞红披风一样。有人推断说斗牛已经成为海明威先生的一项爱好,他为斗牛与西班牙文化、人性、生死的关联而着迷。从某种

透视 PERCEPTION

意义上说，《午后之死》其实是一本关于"原始的西班牙"的书。这种说法还是有一定道理的。海明威先生坦言，他不喜欢"床边神秘主义"那样的写作风格。但是海明威最初的动机可能是：

"斗牛场是战争结束后唯一一个能见证生死、暴卒的地方。我想去西班牙研究斗牛。我努力学习写作，从最简单的开始，其中最简单、最基本的就是暴卒。"

在另一段中，海明威先生指出在热衷斗牛的国家，"人们必须对死亡感兴趣"。他发现卡斯提尔人就对死亡很感兴趣，"每每想要看到死亡降临、逃避死亡、拒绝或接受死亡，人们就会花上一点点钱跑去斗牛场"。然而，英国人和法国人则恰恰相反，"他们为活而生"，所以对斗牛不感兴趣。虽然海明威在说这话时有点神秘兮兮的，但是至少还算不上"床边神秘主义"。

斗牛意味着牛的死亡，因为即使它不死在斗牛场也会在指定的时间内被人在场外屠杀。斗牛同时也意味着马的死亡，海明威说马（刺斗士的坐骑）的死亡最有喜剧色彩，因为它们是因为身上没有垫子保护而死的。斗牛还意味着斗牛士的死亡，不论哪场斗牛，斗牛士都迟早会遍体鳞伤，好的斗牛士每次斗牛表演时都必须游走在死亡边缘。此外，斗牛还意味着优秀的斗牛士必须真正享受死亡；观众必须能够在斗牛表演中获取极致的快感。正如海明威先生所说：

"斗牛士必须从精神上享受杀戮。利落地并且用一种极富美感和尊严的方式将对手干掉，一直都是人类的一种享受方式。一旦你接受了死亡游戏的规则，不可杀戮就是一条简单、自然、可以信守的戒律。但是当人还在抗拒死亡时，他就会迷恋于只有神才会拥有的生杀之权。这是那些享受杀戮的人最深切的快乐。一切都是骄傲地完成的，当然，骄傲是基督教中的七宗罪之一，是异教徒的品质。然而，恰恰是这种骄傲成就了斗牛和以杀戮为乐的优秀斗牛士。"

斗牛迷们真正享受的是公牛的勇敢或者高贵，以及斗牛士的技艺和勇气。至少这是海明威先生所关注的。斗牛迷不想看到优秀的斗牛士死去，尽管当一个无能的斗牛士受伤时他可能熟视无睹，甚至还在这个斗牛士离

〈183〉

开斗牛场时朝他扔瓶子或其他硬物。然而,令人难以置信的是那些对死亡抱有极大兴趣的人有时不希望亲眼看到斗牛士死在公牛手上。海明威先生说斗牛士在紧要关头离牛角越近,表演就越受欢迎。在斗牛场,没有冒险便无技艺可言。作为一个斗牛迷,海明威先生痛恨斗牛士利用虚招杀死公牛,"他应该充分暴露自己的身体,然后利用手中的剑刺死公牛"。就算是最后一下刺得很到位,斗牛士所处的位置也必须很讲究:他必须处在一个在一阵不合时宜的风刮起或者公牛突然抬头时使自己的身体能够被撞伤的位置。如果观众没有感到一种近乎变态的快感,那么斗牛也就跟其他集会没什么两样了。

然而,斗牛的确是一门艺术。海明威将斗牛和雕塑、绘画相提并论一点都不可笑。斗牛士在危急关头所展现的曲线、人与牛的有机融合都能为聪明的斗牛迷带来快感。于是,斗牛成了一种用死来呈现的艺术。观众能够将自己想象为斗牛士,体会对于死亡的恐惧。因为,即使是最优秀的斗牛士也有恐惧的时候,这种恐惧有时会持续数日或数年。

《午后之死》这本书不但小心翼翼地解释了很多斗牛的细节,也为我们展示了斗牛的精神境界。

必须要说的是,海明威一贯的写作风格在《午后之死》一书中并没有那么强烈、明显。在这本书中,海明威犯了一个严重的错误,那就是很多句子令人费解,必须要读上两三遍才能明白。

这本书会出现在海明威迷的书架上。

More to Read

这篇书评发表于1932年9月25日的《纽约时报》。虽然与今世相隔近80年,但是其文字读起来丝毫没有古旧之感。作者就像是一位风度翩翩的文学教授在讲坛上向自己的学生推介着一本令自己爱不释手的新书。无论是《午后之死》的思想性、文化性,还是海明威的语言风格和文字难度,作者都在书评中娓娓道来,而作者的洞察能力也由此可见一斑。对斗牛以及海明威都很感兴趣的读者不妨看看这本《午后之死》。

透 视 PERCEPTION

Reading Guidance

本文作者索尔·贝娄被认为是美国当代最负盛名的作家之一。早期创作有结构优美的《晃来晃去的人》(*Dangling Man*)(1944)、《受害者》(*The Victim*)(1947),颇被评论界瞩目。《奥吉·玛琪历险记》(*The Adventure of Augie March*)(1953)的出版,使他一举成名,并首次获得美国国家图书奖,他在文坛的地位就此确立。1976年,索尔·贝娄获得诺贝尔文学奖,他的作品被认为"融合了对人的理解和对当代文化的精妙分析",瑞典皇家学会在颁奖时特别提及他的小说《抓紧时光》,认为此书是现代典型作品之一。本文论述了严肃文学和以技术为主要载体的大众文化之间的关系。

Hidden Within Technology's Empire, a Republic of Letters

When I was a boy "discovering literature", I used to think how wonderful it would be if every other person on the street were familiar with Proust and Joyce or T. E. Lawrence or Pasternak and Kafka. Later I learned how refractory to high culture the democratic masses were. Lincoln as a young frontiersman read Plutarch, Shakespeare and the Bible. But then he was Lincoln.

For many decades now I have been a fiction writer, and from the first I was aware that mine was a questionable occupation. In the 1930's an elderly neighbor in Chicago told me that he wrote fiction for the pulps. "The people on the block wonder why I don't go to a job, and I'm seen puttering around, trimming the bushes or painting a fence instead of working in a factory. But I'm a writer. I sell to *Argosy* and *Doc Savage*," he said with a certain gloom. "They wouldn't call that a trade." Probably he noticed that I was a bookish boy, likely to sympathize with him, and perhaps he was trying to warn me to avoid being unlike others. But it was too late for that.

From the first, too, I had been warned that the novel was at the point of death, that like the walled city or the crossbow, it was a thing of the past. And no one likes to be at odds with history. Oswald Spengler, one of the most widely read authors of the early 30's, taught that our tired old civilization was very nearly finished. His advice to the young was to avoid literature and the arts and to embrace mechanization and become engineers.

Sixty years later, in a recent issue of *The Wall Street Journal*, I come upon the old Spenglerian argument in a contemporary form. Terry Teachout, unlike Spengler, does not dump paralyzing mountains of historical theory upon us, but there are signs that he has weighed, sifted and pondered the evidence.

He speaks of our "atomized culture", and his is a responsible, up-to-date and carefully considered opinion. He speaks of "art forms as technologies". He tells us that movies will soon be "downloadable"—that is, transferable from one computer to the memory of another device—and predicts that films will soon be marketed like books. He predicts that the near-magical powers of technology are bringing us to the threshold of a new age and concludes, "Once this happens, my guess is that the independent movie will replace the novel as the principal vehicle for serious storytelling in the 21st century."

In support of this argument, Mr. Teachout cites the ominous drop in the volume of book sales and the great increase in movie attendance: "For Americans under the age of 30, film has replaced the novel as the dominant mode of artistic expression." To this Mr. Teachout adds that popular novelists like Tom Clancy and Stephen King "top out at around a million copies per book", and notes, "The final episode of NBC's *Cheers*, by contrast, was seen by 42 million people."

On majoritarian grounds, the movies win. "The power of novels to shape the national conversation has declined," says Mr. Teachout. But I am not at all certain that in their day *Moby-Dick* or *The Scarlet Letter* had any considerable influence on "the national conversation". In the mid-19th century it was *Uncle Tom's Cabin* that impressed the great public. *Moby-Dick* was a small-public novel.

The literary masterpieces of the 20th century were for the most part the work of novelists who had no large public in mind. The novels of Proust and Joyce were written in a cultural twilight and were not intended to be read under the blaze and dazzle of popularity.

Mr. Teachout's article in *The Journal* follows the path generally taken by observers whose aim is to discover a trend. "According to one recent study 55 percent of Americans spend less than 30 minutes reading anything at all... It may even be that movies have superseded novels not because Americans have grown dumber but because the novel is an obsolete artistic technology."

John Cheever told me long ago that it was his readers who kept him going, people from every part of the country who had written to him. When he was at work, he was aware of these readers and correspondents in the woods beyond the lawn. "If I couldn't picture them, I'd be sunk," he said. And the novelist Wright Morris, urging me to get an electric typewriter, said that he seldom turned his machine off. "When I'm not writing, I listen to the electricity," he said. "It keeps me company. We have conversations."

I wonder how Mr. Teachout might square such idiosyncrasies with his "art forms as technologies". Perhaps he would argue that these two writers had

somehow isolated themselves from "broad-based cultural influence". Mr. Teachout has at least one laudable purpose: He thinks that he sees a way to bring together the great public of the movies with the small public of the highbrows. He is, however, interested in millions: millions of dollars, millions of readers, millions of viewers.

There was no rivalry then between the viewer and the reader. Nobody supervised our reading. We were on our own. We civilized ourselves. We found or made a mental and imaginative life. Because we could read, we learned also to write. It did not confuse me to see *Treasure Island* in the movies and then read the book. There was no competition for our attention.

One of the more attractive oddities of the United States is that our minorities are so numerous, so huge. A minority of millions is not at all unusual. But there are in fact millions of literate Americans in a state of separation from others of their kind. They are, if you like, the readers of Cheever, a crowd of them too large to be hidden in the woods. Departments of literature across the country have not succeeded in alienating them from books, works old and new. My friend Keith Botsford and I felt strongly that if the woods were filled with readers gone astray, among those readers there were probably writers as well.

To learn in detail of their existence you have only to publish a magazine like *The Republic of Letters*. Given encouragement, unknown writers, formerly without hope, materialize.

We have no way of guessing how many independent, self-initiated connoisseurs and lovers of literature have survived in remote corners of the country. The little evidence we have suggests that they are glad to find us, they are grateful. They want more than they are getting. Ingenious technology has failed to give them what they so badly need.

透视 PERCEPTION

Notes

refractory：难控制的
transferable：可转移的
encouragement：鼓励

隐匿于技术帝国中的一方文学理想国

当我还只是个"探索文学"的毛头小伙时就总在想,要是街头巷尾人尽皆知普鲁斯特、乔伊斯、托马斯·爱德华·劳伦斯、帕斯捷尔纳克或卡夫卡该多棒啊。后来我才明白民主大众与高雅文化是多么格格不入。当年林肯读普鲁塔克、莎士比亚和《圣经》时,不过只是年纪轻轻的一介边民。可是话又说回来,人家毕竟是林肯。

现在,我从事小说创作已有数十载。起初,我就知道这是个问题职业。20世纪30年代,我在芝加哥的一位年迈的邻居告诉我,他是为通俗刊物创作小说的。"小区的人们都纳闷我为什么不找份工作,他们总是看见我整天游手好闲,不是剪枝掐叶,就是粉刷篱笆,反正是不在工厂干活。可我是作家,还为《商船队》和《萨维奇博士》供稿呢。"他郁郁地说:"唉,可这在他们看来算不上正经职业。"或许,他看我也有点书生气,可能与他惺惺相惜;又或许他是在极力提醒我不要与众不同。不过,为时晚矣。

打开始,就有人警告过我:小说将亡,犹如围城和石弓,已是旧物,没人愿意跟历史较劲。奥斯瓦尔德·斯宾格勒是20世纪30年代初最受读者拥趸的作家之一,他曾教化说,我们疲惫的古老文明几近终结。他给年轻人的忠告是远文学艺术而近机械文明,做工程师。

60年后，我在近期的《华尔街日报》上读到了一篇文章，其内容全然是斯宾格勒理论的旧调"新"弹。与斯宾格勒不同，其作者泰瑞·迪奇奥特并没有将一座座压得人动弹不了的历史理论大山劈头盖脸地砸向我们，他更像是在为历史理论筛选和考量凿凿之据。

他谈及我们的"原子化文化"（译者注：即大众化社会文化），观点负责、新潮而且审慎。他也提到了"艺术形式技术化"。他告诉我们电影很快可以下载观看：即能从一台电脑转移到另一台设备的内存中；并预见电影即将像书籍一样出售。他甚至预言技术近乎魔幻般的力量正引领我们迈入新世纪的门槛，而且断定："一旦如此，我估计独立电影将取代小说，成为21世纪严肃叙事的主要载体。"

迪奇奥特先生还援引书籍销量下滑的不祥之兆和观影者与日"巨"增为证："对于30岁以下的美国人而言，电影已经取代小说成为艺术表现的主导模式。"进而又说汤姆·克兰西和史蒂芬·金等畅销小说家"每部书的销量顶天为100万册左右"，相形之下，"NBC（美国全国广播公司）播出的《干杯》最后一集的观众人数为4200万。"

站在少数服从多数主义者的立场上看，电影确是赢家。迪奇奥特先生说："小说左右国民话语的力量日益下降。"不过，我也说不好当年的《大白鲸》和《红字》对于所谓的"国民话语"到底有多少实质影响。19世纪中期，真正令大众印象深刻的是《汤姆叔叔的小屋》，而《大白鲸》是一部小众小说。

20世纪的文学名著多半出自那些未曾考虑大众趣味的小说家之手。普鲁斯特和乔伊斯的小说创作于文化微茫之际，而无意于在盛名之下被传阅。

迪奇特奥先生在《华尔街日报》上的这篇文章与那些旨在发现潮流的观察家们的路数如出一辙。"最新研究表明，55%的美国人每天阅读时间还不足30分钟……电影之所以取代小说，并不是因为美国人头脑日渐简单，而是因为小说已是过时的技术。"

很久以前，约翰·契弗跟我说，让他笔耕不辍的是他的读者，而且给他写信的人遍及全国各地。写作时，他始终心系树林深处和草坪那边的读者和通信者。他说:"不想着他们,我就高兴不起来。"小说家赖特·莫里斯曾劝我买台电动打字机,他说他很少关上打字机,"即便我不写作时,也要听着电流的声音,它是我的伴儿,我们聊天。"

我想知道迪奇奥特先生如何用所谓的"艺术形式技术化"来解释这些个人癖好。或许,他会争辩说上述两位作家从某种意义上脱离了"基础广泛的文化影响"。迪奇奥特先生写这篇文章倒是至少有一个可以为人称道的良苦用心:即他自认为看到了能够将电影之大众和高雅文化之小众撮合到一起的门径。然而,他所关心的终究只是"数百万"这个数字:数百万美金、数百万读者、数百万观众。

观众与读者之间并无竞争可言。没人监督我们的阅读。我们独立自主、自我教化。我们自己发现、塑造了一个充满想象的精神世界。也正因为能够阅读,我们才学着去写作。先看电影版《金银岛》再看其原著,这不会让我感到不解,二者对于我们关注力并不构成竞争。

美国最吸引人的怪现象之一便是我们的少数派是如此之众,如此之巨。一个少数派哪怕只有几百万人也不足为奇。然而,为数只有几百万人的文学之士却成了异类。可以说,这些人中就有契弗的读者,其人数之多连山林也藏其不住。全国各处的文学系无法将他们与新旧书籍和作品相隔离。我的朋友基斯·博茨福德和我强烈地感到,如果山林中尽是离群索居的读者,那么其间必有作家。

为了能够详尽地了解他们的生存状态,你只要出版一本类似我们的《文学理想国》这样的刊物即可。一旦受到鼓舞,那些默默无闻、心灰意冷的作家也会现身。

我们无法猜测究竟有多少独立、自发的文学内行及其爱好者隐逸在偏远一隅。从我们所掌握的这一点证据来看,他们愿意找到我们,并对此心存感激,他们也还想继续看我们的刊物。新奇的技术未能满足他们对文学的渴望。

More to Read

  选择此文的目的有两个。其一,本文的立意深刻,为我们阐释了大众文化与严肃文化之间的关系。一方面,电影、电视剧等大众文化的发展从某种程度上说成为大众与严肃文学之间的鸿沟。忙碌的现代生活,让人们更乐于亲近所谓的"快餐文化",深刻的东西让人觉得更辛苦,倒不如一笑了之来得轻松愉快。也许,"人类一思考,上帝就发笑"。另一方面,电影、电视剧有时也缩短了人们与严肃文学之间的距离。且看中国出现的古典名著翻拍热就明白了。在国外,名著也时常被搬上大银幕,《飘》、《傲慢与偏见》、《百万英镑》等等。恐怕,很多中国人也是通过电影才想到去读原作吧! 其二,此文的逻辑非常缜密。作者索尔·贝娄虽然以小说著称,但是从这篇议论文章可以看出他文笔的犀利,头脑的冷静,思维的缜密。作者虽没有使用太多华丽的辞藻,但是字字句句读起来却铿锵有力,论证环环相扣、干净利落,行文之美顷刻可见。